SpringerBriefs in Computer Science

Series Editors
Stan Zdonik
Peng Ning
Shashi Shekhar
Jonathan Katz
Xindong Wu
Lakhmi C Jain
David Padua
Xuemin Shen
Borko Furht

For further volumes:
http://www.springer.com/series/10028

Xiao Liu · Dong Yuan · Gaofeng Zhang
Wenhao Li · Dahai Cao · Qiang He
Jinjun Chen · Yun Yang

The Design of Cloud Workflow Systems

 Springer

Xiao Liu
Dong Yuan
Gaofeng Zhang
Wenhao Li
Dahai Cao
Qiang He
Jinjun Chen
Yun Yang
Faculty of Information and Communication
  Technologies
Centre for Computing and Engineering
  Software Systems
Swinburne University of Technology
Hawthorn, Melbourne, VIC 3122
Australia

Xiao Liu
e-mail: xliu@swin.edu.au

Dong Yuan
e-mail: dyuan@swin.edu.au

Gaofeng Zhang
e-mail: gzhang@swin.edu.au

Wenhao Li
e-mail: wli@swin.edu.au

Dahai Cao
e-mail: dcao@swin.edu.au

Qiang He
e-mail: heqiang@gmail.com

Yun Yang
e-mail: yyang@swin.edu.au

Jinjun Chen
Faculty of Engineering and Information
Technology
Centre for Innovation in IT Services and
Applications
University of Technology
Sydney, NSW 2007
Australia
e-mail: jinjun.chen@gmail.com

ISSN 2191-5768   e-ISSN 2191-5776
ISBN 978-1-4614-1932-7   e-ISBN 978-1-4614-1933-4
DOI 10.1007/978-1-4614-1933-4
Springer New York Dordrecht Heidelberg London

Library of Congress Control Number: 2011940815

Printed on acid-free paper

Springer is part of Springer Science+Business Media (www.springer.com)

Preface

Cloud computing is the latest computing paradigm which brings entirely new innovations to the Information Technology (IT) industry. Gartner estimated the demand in 2009 for cloud computing at \$46 billion, rising to \$150 billion by 2013.[1] According to Microsoft, cloud computing can help their customers to save up to 80% on the cost of their IT infrastructure.[2]

Workflow systems have been widely used as software tools to support process automation, and also as middleware services for distributed high performance computing infrastructures such as cluster, peer-to-peer, and grid computing. In the upcoming few years, given the enormous market of cloud computing, there will be a rapid growth of software as a service (SaaS), and we can envisage that cloud workflow system can be one of the competitive software platforms to support the design, development and running of cloud based software applications.

Cloud computing has many unique characteristics such as its organisation and delivery of computing resources, but it also inherits and shares many aspects with other existing computing paradigms such as grid computing, utility computing and service computing. Therefore, to design and develop a cloud workflow system, it is essential to investigate the system fundamentals such as the system architecture, functionality and quality of service (QoS), while in the meantime, compare the differences and similarities in the system requirements to determine whether existing strategies can be adopted and/or adapted for the new scenario, or entirely new system designs are required.

This book is written to discuss and address these timely issues. Since cloud computing as well as cloud workflow system is evolving in a fast pace, this book only reflects the view of the authors based on their best knowledge about the current situation, and demonstrates the research progress and outcomes. It is neither the only view nor the unanimous view about cloud workflow systems. Nevertheless, after reading this book, readers are expected to have a basic idea about what is a cloud workflow system, and what are the key factors in its design.

---

[1] http://www.gartner.com/DisplayDocument?doc_cd=166525&ref=g_SiteLink

[2] http://www.microsoft.com/presspass/presskits/cloud/docs/The-Economics-of-the-Cloud.pdf

Acknowledgments

We are grateful for the discussions with Mr. Zhangjun Wu and his colleagues from HuaAn Securities on the securities exchange business process, and Dr. Willem van Straten and Ms. Lina Levin from Swinburne Centre for Astrophysics and Super-computing for the pulsar searching scientific workflow. The authors would also like to thank Ms. Jennifer Maurer from Springer for her help during the preparation of this book. This work is partially supported by Australian Research Council under Linkage Project LP0990393 and Discovery Project DP110101340, as well as State Administration of Foreign Experts Affairs of China Project P201100001, and the National Natural Science Foundation of China under grant No. 61170192.

Contents

About the Authors

Xiao Liu received his Ph.D. degree in Computer Science and Software Engineering from the Faculty of Information and Communication Technologies at Swinburne University of Technology, Melbourne, Australia in 2011. He received his Master and Bachelor degree from the School of Management, Hefei University of Technology, Hefei, China, in 2007 and 2004 respectively, all in Information Management and Information System. He is currently a postdoctoral research fellow in the Centre of Computing and Engineering Software System at Swinburne University of Technology. His research interests include workflow management systems, scientific workflow, business process management and quality of service.

Dong Yuan received the Bachelor degree in 2005 and Master degree in 2008 both from Shandong University, Jinan, China, all in Computer Science. He is currently a Ph.D. student in the Faculty of Information and Communication Technologies at Swinburne University of Technology, Melbourne, Australia. His research interests include data management in workflow systems, scheduling and resource management, grid and cloud computing.

Gaofeng Zhang received the Bachelor and Master degrees in Computer Science from Hefei University of Technology, Hefei, China, in 2005 and 2008 respectively. He is currently working toward the Ph.D. degree in Information and Communication Technology under the supervision of A/Prof. Jinjun Chen and Prof. Yun Yang in Faulty of Information and Communication Technologies, Swinburne University of Technology, Melbourne, Australia. His research interests include privacy protection strategy, risk evaluation, and security mechanism in cloud computing.

Wenhao Li obtained his Bachelor and Master degree of Engineering from Shan Dong University in China in 2007 and 2010 respectively. He participated in a program funds by National Natural Science Foundation of China during his postgraduate studies and published several papers in national and international journals. He is currently a first-year Ph.D. candidate in Faculty of Information and Communication Technologies, Swinburne University of Technology, supervised by Prof. Yun Yang and A/Prof. Jinjun Chen. He's research interests include parallel and distributed computing, cloud and grid computing, workflow technologies and data management in distributed computing environment.

Dahai Cao received his master degree in software engineering from Tsinghua University, Beijing, China, 2005. He is currently a Ph.D. student in Swinburne University Centre for Computing and Engineering Software Systems, Melbourne, Australia. His research interests include cloud-based large-scale workflow management systems, adaptive workflow management and cloud computing.

Qiang He received his first Ph.D. degree in information and communication technology from Swinburne University of Technology (SUT), Australia, in 2009 and his second Ph.D. degree in computer science and engineering from Huazhong University of Science and Technology (HUST), China, in 2010. He is now a research fellow at SUT. His research interests include services computing, cloud computing, P2P system, workflow management and agent technologies.

Jinjun Chen received his Ph.D. degree in Computer Science and Software Engineering from Swinburne University of Technology, Melbourne, Australia in 2007. He is currently an associate Professor in the Faculty of Engineering and Information Technology, University of Technology, Sydney, Australia. His research interests include Scientific workflow management and applications, workflow management and applications in Web service or SOC environments, workflow management and applications in grid (service)/cloud computing environments, software verification and validation in workflow systems, QoS and resource scheduling in distributed computing systems such as cloud computing, service oriented computing, semantics and knowledge management, cloud computing.

Yun Yang received a Master of Engineering degree from The University of Science and Technology of China, Hefei, China, in 1987, and a Ph.D. degree from The University of Queensland, Brisbane, Australia, in 1992, all in computer science. He is currently a full Professor in the Faculty of Information and Communication Technologies at Swinburne University of Technology, Melbourne, Australia. Prior to joining Swinburne as an Associate Professor in late 1999, he was a Lecture and Senior Lecturer at Deakin University during 1996–1999. Before that, he was a Research Scientist at DSTC—Cooperative Research Centre for Distributed Systems Technology during 1993–1996. He also worked at Beihang University in China during 1987–1988. He has published more than 200 papers on journals and refereed conferences. His research interests include software engineering; p2p, grid and cloud computing; workflow systems; service-oriented computing; Internet computing applications; and CSCW.

Introduction

Workflow systems originated from office automation which started in 1970s to support the office information management for accomplishing simple business tasks [2]. In the last decade, workflow systems become more oriented to the process automation of large scale business and scientific applications. Many workflow systems have been deployed on high performance computing infrastructures such as cluster, peer-to-peer (p2p), and grid computing [59, 77, 85]. One of the driving forces is the increasing demand of large scale instance intensive and data/computation intensive workflow applications (large scale workflow applications for short) which are common in both e-business and e-science application areas. Typical examples include such as the instance intensive securities exchange process in a stock market, the flight booking process in a travel agency; and the data and computation intensive pulsar searching process in Astrophysics, the weather forecast process in Meteorology. These large scale workflow applications normally require the support of powerful high performance computing infrastructures (e.g. advanced CPU units, large memory space and high speed network).

To meet these high resource requirements, expensive computing infrastructures including such as supercomputers, data servers and fibre networks are purchased, installed, and maintained by system users with huge on-going capital investment. However, the problems of resource scalability and elasticity still exist in the conventional computing paradigm. Since most of these resources are self-contained and organised in a heterogeneous way, resource scalability is very low. Due to such a problem, it incurs great cost, if not impossible, to recruit external resources to address 'resource insufficiency' during peak times. Meanwhile, since in current computing paradigms, workflow systems have to maintain their own computing resources rather than employ them from or deliver them to third parties, resource elasticity is very poor. Due to such a problem, most of the computing resources during off-peak times are largely idle, and thus results in the low ROI (return on investment) and a giant waste of energy consumption [58, 64].

In recent years, cloud computing is emerging as the latest distributed computing paradigm and attracts increasing interests of researchers in the area of Distributed and Parallel Computing [65], Service Oriented Computing [7] and Software

Engineering [70]. As proposed by Ian Foster in [32] and shared by many researchers and practitioners, compared with conventional computing paradigms, cloud computing can provide "a pool of abstracted, virtualised, dynamically-scalable, managed computing power, storage, platforms, and services are delivered on demand to external customers over the Internet". Therefore, cloud computing can provide scalable resources on demand to system requirement. Meanwhile, cloud computing adopts market-oriented business model where users are charged according to the usage of cloud services such as computing, storage and network services like conventional utilities in everyday life (e.g. water, electricity, gas and telephony) [17]. Evidently, it is possible to utilise cloud computing to address the problems of resource scalability and elasticity for managing large scale workflow applications. Therefore, the investigation of workflow systems based on cloud computing, namely cloud workflow systems, is a timely issue and worthwhile for increasing efforts.

This book discusses the design of cloud workflow systems, and focuses on three fundamental aspects, viz. system architecture, functionality and quality of service (QoS management). In this book, through the investigation of the new cloud computing paradigm and the conventional workflow systems, we emphasise on the reuse and adaptation of existing methodologies and strategies rather than build from the scratch.

This book consists of five chapters.

Chapter 1 presents an overview about cloud computing and workflow systems. Two motivating examples each for an e-science and e-business application are also illustrated.

Chapter 2 introduces the system architecture where both the general cloud software architecture and the general cloud workflow system architecture are presented.

Chapter 3 discusses the cloud workflow system functionality which is organised and designed based on the classical workflow reference model.

Chapter 4 presents the QoS management in cloud workflow systems where the basic requirements and strategies for performance management, data storage management, data replication management and privacy protection are discussed.

Finally, Chap. 5 demonstrates a case study on our SwinDeW-C cloud workflow system to illustrate the implementation of the system design and demonstrate some evaluation results.

The Appendices include the detailed strategies and algorithms, and the literature review of some related studies.

This book can be used as a reference for both researchers and practitioners who are interested in the design, development and application of cloud workflow systems.

Chapter 1
Workflow Systems in the Cloud

In this chapter, we will present an overview about the background of cloud computing and workflow systems. Specifically, Sect. 1.1 introduces the novel cloud computing paradigm. Section 1.2 reviews the workflow systems, especially in the distributed computing environments. Section 1.3 introduces the cloud workflow systems. In Sect. 1.4, we demonstrate two motivating examples, one for large-scale data and computation intensive e-science application in Astrophysics and one for instance intensive e-business application in the stock market. Finally, Sect. 1.5 points out the key issue in the design of cloud workflow systems.

1.1 Background: Cloud Computing

In late 2007 the concept of cloud computing was proposed [8, 16, 79]. Cloud computing, nowadays widely considered as the "next generation" of Information Technology (IT), is a new paradigm offering virtually unlimited, cheap, readily available, "utility type" computing resources as services via the Internet. As very high network bandwidth becomes available it has become possible to envisage all the resources needed to accomplish IT functions as residing on the Internet rather than physically existing on the users' premises. A cloud computing platform is made up of a—possibly widely dispersed—set of computing hardware platforms networked together and running a number of diverse software services. With effective facilitation of cloud computing many sophisticated software applications can be further advanced to stretch their limits and yet with reduced running costs and energy consumption. The advantages of cloud computing, especially its software as a service (SaaS) and utility computing, enable entirely new innovations to the design and development of software applications [1, 58]. It is generally agreed among many researchers and practitioners that cloud applications are the future trend for business software applications since SaaS can provide massive

X. Liu et al., *The Design of Cloud Workflow Systems*,
SpringerBriefs in Computer Science, DOI: 10.1007/978-1-4614-1933-4_1,
© The Author(s) 2012

software services with different capabilities and utility computing can provide unlimited on-demand computing power. Successful stories include New York Times which turns 11 million archived articles into pdf files in only one day using cloud software, Hadoop, and computing power on Amazon's cloud [36]. Another one is Animoto which employs Amazon's cloud to deal with nearly 750,000 new registered users in three days and 25,000 people online user at the peak time [12].

Gartner estimated the demand in 2009 for cloud computing at $46 billion, rising to $150 billion by 2013 [34]. Compared to previous computing infrastructures, cloud computing has attractive features such as lower cost, greater resource sharing, more scalability and better reliability. In addition to the cost reduction on the infrastructure, energy consumption for the infrastructures can also be significantly reduced. International governments such as the United States, the United Kingdom, Canada, Australian and New Zealand governments, all take cloud services as an opportunity to improve business outcomes through eliminating redundancy, increasing agility and providing ICT services at a potentially cheaper cost [1, 10].

The Australian Government's business operations are highly dependent on ICT which estimated costs around $4.3 billion per annum according to the Financial Management and Accountability Australian government agencies, research institutes, and enterprises have initiated investigations and strategic plans to grasp the opportunities and understand the challenges brought by cloud computing. Cloud computing has been included in the Australian Government ICT Sustainability Plan 2010–2015 as an energy efficient technology for the Australian Government Data Centre Strategy [11]. The Department of Finance and Deregulation has drafted the Cloud Computing Strategic Direction Paper [10], in which it has mentioned that Sir Peter Gershon (who undertook the review of Australian Government's use of ICT) estimated that costs of $1 billion could be avoided by developing a data centre strategy for the next 15 years. Many Australian government agencies such as Australian Taxation Office (ATO), Department of Immigration and Citizenship (DIAC), West Australian Department of Treasure and Finance (DTF), and Australian Maritime Safety Authority (AMSA), have announced their progress in either the development stage or the proof of concept stage for cloud applications. The Australian Academy of Technological Sciences and Engineering (ATSE) have written a report to discuss the opportunities and challenges for Australian government, universities and business [1]. Enterprises such as Westpac, Telstra, MYOB, Commonwealth Bank, Australian and New Zealand Banking Group (ANZ) and SAP have also announced their initiatives and investment plans to support the migration and running of their business applications in the cloud.

Given the enormous amount of upcoming investment on cloud infrastructures, successful design and development of cloud software applications for government and business services are required to exhibit the benefits, reveal the difficulties, and stimulate the fast development of the cloud market.

1.2 Background: Workflow Systems

The Workflow Management Coalition (WfMC) defined a workflow as "the auto-mation of a business process, in whole or part, during which documents, information or tasks are passed from one participant to another for action, according to a set of procedural rules" [82].

A workflow system is a system that completely defines, manages and executes "workflows" through the execution of software whose order of execution is driven by a computer representation of the workflow logic. In general, a workflow system belongs to a type of information system for the management of business processes. The history of workflow system begins in the 1970s when Ellis and others worked at Xerox PARC on "Office Automation Systems" [2]. It only becomes a major tool for business process management and Business Process Redesign (BPR) until 1990s with the popularity of network and component based software systems. One of the most important advantages of workflow system is the separation of functions from applications. In this way, information systems can be made component-based, by first configuring the components and then integrating them [27, 74]. By introducing the workflow schema into an enterprise's information system, business agility can be greatly enhanced. The basic idea is very similar to the input of a database schema for software systems.

In the last two decades, workflow systems have been evolved with the fast growth of distributed computing [26]. In the earlier stage, client–server is the most dominant architecture for workflow systems. This architecture has the advantages such as thin clients, centralised monitoring and auditing, simple synchronisation mechanisms, one copy of process state, and ease of design, implementation and deployment for workflows. However, it also faces conspicuous difficulties like low performance, reliability and scalability. Some typical client–server workflow management systems: Exotica/FMDC [5], ADEPT (http://www.adepttech.com/workflow.php), DartFlow [18], and METUFlow [28].

Peer-to-peer workflow management systems abandon the dominating client–server architecture and use the peer-to-peer infrastructure to provide decentralised workflow support. As the workflow functions are fulfilled through the direct communication and coordination among the relevant peers, performance bottle-necks are likely to be eliminated whilst increased resilience to failure and enhanced scalability are likely to be achieved. Here are some typical peer-to-peer workflow management systems are RainMan [63], Serendipity-II [37] and SwinDeW [84].

The last decade has seen a significant development of distributed workflow systems and scientific workflow systems with the grid computing paradigm. The workflow enactment service of grid workflow management systems may be built on top of the low level grid middleware (e.g. Globus toolkit (http://www.globus.org/toolkit/), UNICORE (http://www.unicore.eu/) and Alchemi (http://www.cloudbus.org/∼alchemi/), through which the workflow management system invokes services provided by grid resources [87]. At both the build-time and runtime stages, the information about resources and applications may need to be retrieved using grid information services. There are many grid workflow management systems currently, and here we only list several representative grid workflow systems which are in use recently. These systems include ASKALON (http://www.askalon.org/), GrADS (http://www.iges.org/grads/) , GridAnt (http://www.globus.org/cog/projects/gridant/), Gridbus (http://www.gridbus.org/), GridFlow (http://gridflow.ca/), Kepler (https://kepler-project.org/), Pegasus (http://pegasus.isi.edu/), Taverna (http://www.taverna.org.uk/) and Triana (http://www.trianacode.org/). The details of these workflow management systems can be found in their respective references. In [87], comparisons of several representative Grid workflow systems are given in aspects of (1) scheduling architecture, (2) decision making, (3) planning scheme, (4) scheduling strategy, and (5) performance estimation.

1.3 Cloud Workflow Systems

With the emerging of the latest cloud computing paradigm, the trend for distributed workflow systems is shifting to cloud computing based workflow systems, or cloud workflow systems for short. Given the advantages of cloud computing, cloud workflow systems can be widely used as platform softwares (or middleware services) to facilitate the usage of cloud services. For example, cloud workflow systems can support many complex e-science applications such as climate modelling, earthquake modelling, weather forecast, Astrophysics and high energy physics [27]. These e-science applications are typically data and computation intensive which require MapReduce-like large scale parallel and distributed processing in the cloud. Meanwhile, cloud workflow systems can also support many e-business applications such as journey planning (e.g. flight and hotel bookings), stock exchange, insurance claim, bank transactions and business to customer (B2C) trading in e-commerce [83]. These e-business applications are typically instance and transaction intensive during the peak hours which require easy-scale and dynamic provision of computing resources in the cloud. The increasing popularity of cloud workflow systems lies in the mutual benefits between workflow systems and cloud in nature, to be more specifically:

1) Cloud brings workflow systems with a large number of easy access and powerful software and hardware services to support their extensive applications. The merit of a workflow system is that users can build up their applications with visual modelling (e.g. Petri Net or DAG based modelling tools) instead of sophisticated and time-consuming programming [2]. Workflow execution engines can understand workflow specifications (also named as workflow templates which may consist of task definitions, process structures and other functional or non-functional constraints) created by users and invoke corresponding software (e.g. remote Web services and/or local software programs) to execute workflow tasks in an automatic and coordinated fashion. However, one of the major

problems that hinder the extensive application of workflow systems is the lack of easy access of software components. Therefore, workflow systems need the cloud to serve as an easy access of resource pool to provide a large number of powerful software services. In fact, given the increasing demand of global economy, there are already significant numbers of research and development on distributed Web-service based workflow systems to support business and scientific processes [1, 30].

2) Workflow systems bring the cloud with a type of visual-programmable platform/middleware services to facilitate the easy use of cloud services [54]. With the rapid growth of the cloud market, there will be increasing number of cloud service providers. However, one of the obstacles for building software applications in the cloud is the access and composition of cloud services. Therefore, cloud platform/middleware services which provide programming like environments for the access and composition of cloud services play a significant role in cloud software development. However, most consumers in the cloud market are not IT professionals (e.g. scientists and businesspeople in non-IT areas), and usually they do not acquire sufficient knowledge for sophisticated programming. Workflow systems, as a type of visual-programmable platform/middleware services, can relieve users from traditional programming with visual modelling tools (or slight help of scripting language in some cases) [2]. Therefore, the cloud needs workflow systems to serve as a as a type of platform/middleware services to enhance the usability of cloud services, which is the key to promote the benefit of the cloud market. Furthermore, with the increasing size of the cloud market, cloud workflow systems can become efficient tools for the development of quality software applications in the cloud.

In cloud workflow systems, e-science and e-business processes can be modelled or redesigned as cloud workflow specifications at build-time modelling stage [27, 49]. Workflow specifications may contain task definitions for a large number of workflow activities and their non-functional quality of service (QoS) requirements such as performance, reliability and security [87]. Then, at runtime instantiation stage, based on the searching and negotiation capabilities of cloud resource brokers, a set of software and hardware services in the cloud will be selected and reserved which can satisfy the workflow specifications. Finally, at runtime execution stage, cloud workflow instances are executed by employing the underlying cloud software and/or infrastructure services.

Due to the relative new appearance of cloud computing, there are very few publications thus far on cloud workflow management systems though we are aware that many researchers are working in this area at the moment. Besides our work on the SwinDeW-C cloud workflow system [54], the following pieces of work involve executing workflows in the clouds. In [75], Aneka is used as a cloud middleware on which the Gridbus workflow management system deploys and manages job execution. Hoffa et al. explore the differences between running scientific workflows in the cloud and running them on the grid, using Montage (http://montage.ipac.caltech.edu/) on top of the Pegasus-WMS software (http://pegasus.isi.edu/).

1.4 Motivating Examples

In this section, we illustrate two motivating examples to introduce the typical features of both data and computation intensive e-science application and instance intensive e-business application.

A. Example Data/Computation Intensive Scientific Workflow: A Pulsar Searching Workflow

Swinburne Astrophysics group has been conducting pulsar searching surveys using the observation data from Parkes Radio Telescope, which is one of the most famous radio telescopes in the world (http://www.parkes.atnf.csiro.au/). Pulsar searching is a typical data and computation intensive scientific application. It contains complex and time consuming activities and needs to process terabytes of data. Figure 1.1 depicts the high level structure of a pulsar searching workflow, which runs on Swinburne high performance supercomputing facility (http://astronomy.swin.edu.au/supercomputing/).

There are three major steps in the pulsar searching workflow:

(1) Data recording and initial processing. In Parkes Radio Telescope, there are 13 embedding beam receivers, by which signal from the universe are received. The raw signal data are recorded at a rate of one gigabyte per second by the ATNF (http://www.atnf.csiro.au/) Parkes Swinburne Recorder (http://astronomy.swin.edu.au/pulsar/?topic=apsr). Depending on different areas in the universe that the scientists want to conduct the pulsar searching survey, the observation time is normally around 1 h. The raw observation data recorded from the telescope includes the data from multiple beams interleaved. They are processed by a local cluster in Parkes in real time, where different beam files are extracted from the raw data files and compressed. The size of each beam file normally ranges from 1 to 20 GB depending on the observation time. The beam files are archived in tapes for permanent storage and future analysis.

(2) Data preparation for pulsar seeking. Scientists analyse the beam files to find potentially contained pulsar signals. However, the signals are dispersed by the interstellar medium, where scientists have to conduct a *De-dispersion* step to counteract this effect. Since the potential dispersion source is unknown, a large number of de-dispersion files need to be generated with different dispersion trials. For one dispersion trial of one beam file, the size of de-dispersion file is 4.6 MB to approximately 80 MB depending on the size of the input beam file. In the current pulsar searching survey, 1,200 is the minimum number of the dispersion trials, where the *De-dispersion* activity takes around 13 h to finish and generate 90 GB of de-dispersion files. Furthermore, for binary pulsar searching, every de-dispersion file needs another step of processing named *Accelerate*. This step generates the accelerated de-dispersion files with the similar size in the last *De-dispersion* step.

(3) Pulsar seeking process. Based on the generated de-dispersion files, different seeking algorithms can be applied to search pulsar candidates, such as *FFT* (Fast Fourier Transform) *Seeking*, *FFA* (Fast Fold Algorithm) *Seeking*, and *Single Pulse*

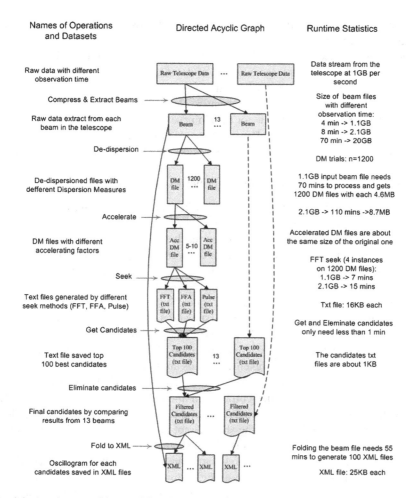

Fig. 1.1 A pulsar searching workflow in astrophysics

Seeking. For example, the *FFT Seeking* takes around 80 min to seek the 1200 de-dispersion files with the size of 90 GB. A candidate list of pulsars is generated after the seeking step which is saved in a 1 KB text file. Furthermore, by comparing the candidates generated from different beam files in the same time session, interference may be detected and some candidates may be eliminated. With the final pulsar candidates, we need to go back to the de-dispersion files to find their feature signals and fold them to XML files. Each candidate is saved in a separated XML file about 25 KB in size. The *Fold to XML* activity takes close to one hour depending on the number of candidates found in this searching process. At last, the XML files are visually displayed to scientists for making decisions on whether a pulsar is found or not.

B. Example Instance Intensive Business Workflow: A Securities Exchange Workflow

The securities exchange workflow is a typical instance-intensive workflow process which involves a large number of transactions and each of them is a relatively short workflow instance with only a few steps. Some steps of the workflow instance are executed concurrently. The example illustrated in Fig. 1.2 is the securities exchange workflow for the Chinese Shanghai A-Share Stock Market (http://www.sse.com.cn/sseportal/en/). There are more than one hundred securities corporations in this market and each corporation may have more than one hundred branches.

There are six major stages in the securities exchange workflow:

(1) The first stage is "client entrustment" (Step 1). Every trading day, there are millions of clients online at the same time and everyone is a potential deal maker. The number of transactions can reach several millions per second at the peak time and the average is around several thousands. Entrustments are processed concurrently in more than 4,000 branches scattered across the country.

(2) The second stage is "fit and make deal" (Step 2 to Step 3). The raw entrustment data from clients are first validated at the corporation level to check whether the clients have enough money to make the deal and whether the deal is feasible (Step 2). After validation, the entrustments will be sent to the stock market where all the entrustments are fit to form the final valence and clinch a deal according to the trading rules. The fitting results are recorded into the database in the securities corporation and fed back to the clients (Step 3). The trading process is completed in several minutes. However, so far, the deal is technically completed but the share is not legally owned by the client until the completion of the entire workflow instance.

(3) The third stage is "register shares variation and calculate capital variation" (Step 4 to Step 6). After 3:00 pm of the trading day, the market is closed to all clients. At this time, all the completed deals need to be archived and to be summed up by securities corporations for clearing. The size of the output file is about 50G with tens of millions of transactions and the duration of the procedure is about 1.5 h (Step 4). After that, the corresponding fees and the credit and debit balance of every corporation are calculated. The size of the output file is about 50 M with several hundred thousands transactions and the duration is about 0.5 h (Step 5). Now all the trading data are transferred to Shanghai Stock Depository and Clearing Corporation of China (http://www.chinaclear.cn/). Registration shares variation of every client and calculation of the capital variation of every client are fulfilled at this stage. Registration ensures that the exchange occurred during the day is legal and the varied amount is registered on the client's account. Calculation of the capital variation ensures that every corporation has the legal evidence to transfer money between firms and branches, or between branches and clients (Step 6).

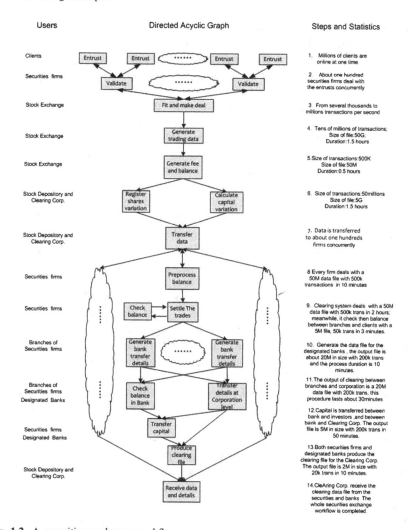

Fig. 1.2 A securities exchange workflow

These are the two main data flow of stock exchange, one is the shares flow, and the other is the capital flow.

(4) The fourth stage is "settle the trades" (Step 7 to Step 9). The output files of the last step are divided by corporation ID and delivered to the securities firms concurrently (Step 7). The subsequent clearing steps are executed at the corporation level which can be processed concurrently among all the corporations. There are three levels of clearings: the first level clearing refers to the clearing between the Clearing Corporation and securities firms, the second one refers to the clearing between securities firms and branches, and the third one refers to the clearing between branches and clients. After the corporation

receives the clearing data files, there are two copies of the trading data in the clearing system. One comes from the database in the securities corporation and the other is from the Clearing Corporation. First, the *Pre-process* should be done to check whether there is any difference between these two files and ensures the first level clearing is correct. If they match, the clearing procedure can start, otherwise, the problem of causing this difference should be fixed before the next level of clearing. The *Pre-process* deals with a 50 M size data file with about 500 k transactions in roughly 10 min (Step 8). Clearing is fulfilled in the clearing system, and it deals with a 50 M size data file with 500 k transactions in 2 h; meanwhile, it checks the balance between branches and clients with a 5 M size data file, 50 k transactions in 3 min. There is a check point between the second level clearing and the third level clearing. The share and capital balance of each branch in the data file from Clearing Corporation should agree with the sum of clients' transactions in the recorded database. Otherwise, manual intervention needs to be conducted after the whole clearing process is completes (Step 9).

(5) The fifth stage is "transfer capital" (Step 10 to Step 12). The output of the second and third level clearing is the money transfer details for each client who made deals during the day. It is a 20 M size data file with 200 k transactions and it should be sent to the designated banks. Meanwhile, this file can also be used to produce the capital transfer details on the corporation level, i.e., which designated bank should transfer how much money to the Clearing Corporation. This procedure lasts for around 10 min (Step 10). The designated banks check the bills in about 30 min on both the client level and the branch level to ensure each entity has enough money to pay for the shares. The input data file is 20 M in size with 200 k transactions. Generally speaking, clients will not be lack of money for the bills because they have been checked before the exchanges occur (Step 11). If the branch is lack of money, certain amount of money is transferred from its deposit automatically. Then the capital is transferred between banks and clients and between banks and the Clearing Corporation. The input file for this step is a 5 M data file with 200 k transactions and it will take around 50 min to completed (Step 12).

(6) The last stage is "produce clearing files" (Step 13 to Step 14). Both securities firms and designated banks should produce the clearing files for the Clearing Corporation. This file includes the transferred details and some statistics. It is about 2 M in size with 20 k records and takes around 10 min (Step 13). The Clearing Corporation receives the clearing data file from the securities firms and banks concurrently. The balance of all the capital transferred is zero at the Clearing Corporation level. Otherwise, exception handling should be conducted with manual intervention (Step 14). The whole securities exchange workflow is completes afterwards.

1.5 Key Issues in the Design of Cloud Workflow Systems

System architecture and its functionalities are the two basic targets for a system design. Since cloud workflow system is a type of workflow system running in the cloud computing environment, its system architecture follows the cloud computing paradigm and its functionalities include the general workflow system functional components and extensions for cloud computing. Additionally, due to the dynamic and the market-oriented nature of cloud computing, quality of service (QoS) management plays an important role in the running of cloud workflow systems. Therefore, quality of service is also considered as a key issue in the design of cloud workflow systems.

1) System architecture: software system architecture design is one of the most important initial steps in the software development process. The system architecture decides how the system components are organised and how they interface with each other. Meanwhile, as discussed in [31], non-functional requirements are not only influenced by individual system components, but also affected by the system architecture. For cloud workflow systems, the system architecture should follow the general architecture of cloud software, but it also needs to be adapted according to different system requirements. The details will be provided in Chap. 3.

2) Functionality: system functionality is a set of system functional components which are designed and developed to meet the system functional requirements. The system functionality of cloud workflow systems can be classified to two major groups, viz. the group of functional components which realises the basic functionality of workflow systems, the group of functional components which realises the management of cloud computing resources. The details will be provided in Chap. 4.

3) Quality of service: QoS management focuses on non-functional requirements which are the constraints on the system functionality such as performance, reliability and security. In a dynamic system environment such as cloud computing, QoS management is critical to ensure the usability of software systems. If without a set of effective QoS management strategies, the customer satisfaction will not be guaranteed, and in most serious cases, the whole system is unusable at all. In cloud workflow systems, typical QoS management tasks may include the performance management, cost management, reliability management and security management. The details will be provided in Chap. 5.

Chapter 2
Cloud Workflow System Architecture

In this chapter, we will present the general cloud workflow system architecture. System architecture in general decides how the system components are organised in different layers and how they communicate with each other. In Sect. 2.1, we will first introduce the general cloud software architecture. Afterwards, Sect. 2.2 will present the general architecture of cloud workflow system. Meanwhile, for each of the general architecture, the concrete architecture of a commercial system is also demonstrated.

2.1 General Cloud Software Architecture

2.1.1 Cloud Architecture

There is so far no unanimous cloud software architecture. Nevertheless, in comparison to the conventional five-layer grid architecture, Ian Foster et al. proposed a representative four-layer architecture for cloud computing which has been accepted by many researchers and practitioners (see Fig. 2.1) [32].

The fabric layer consists of the raw hardware resources, such as the basic computing units, storage disks, and network bandwidths. Similar to grid computing, at this layer, most resources are heterogenous. For example, in a cloud data centre, the underlying physical machines can be commodity PCs, workstations, and supercomputers.

The unified resource layer consists of heterogeneous resources which are usually in the form of virtualised resources. In this layer, the underlying physical machines have been abstracted/encapsulated usually by virtualisation tools so that they can be exposed to upper layer and end users as integrated resources, for example, a virtual computer/cluster, a logical file system, a database system, and so on.

X. Liu et al., *The Design of Cloud Workflow Systems*,
SpringerBriefs in Computer Science, DOI: 10.1007/978-1-4614-1933-4_2,
© The Author(s) 2012

Fig. 2.1 General cloud
software architecture [32]

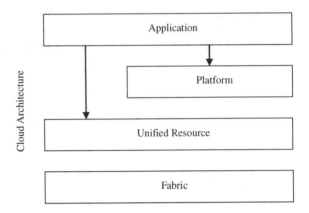

The platform layer consists of a set of resource management tools and middleware services on top of the unified resources. The platform layer can provide a development and/or deployment platform, for example, a Web hosting environment, a workflow modelling service, and a scheduling service, and so on.

Finally, the application layer consists of the user applications which can be any kind of applications such as cloud workflow applications, social networking tools, and e-commerce websites.

2.1.2 Example: Aneka Cloud Architecture

Figure 2.1 provides a high level abstract view of the general cloud software architecture. To illustrate it further additional details, we take the Aneka cloud as an example. Aneka project (http://www.manjrasoft.com/products.html) developed in the Cloud Computing and Distributed Systems (CLOUDS) Lab, University of Melbourne, is a software platform and a framework for developing distributed applications on the cloud. Aneka has now been commercialised by Manjrasoft Pty Ltd (http://www.manjrasoft.com/) as a technology to enable.NET-based enterprise cloud computing. As shown in Fig. 2.2, the fabric layer of Aneka cloud can contain the physical resources in the private cloud and virtualised resources in the public cloud provided by such as Amazon, IBM or Microsoft. The unified resource layer and the platform layer are represented by the Platform Abstraction Layer (PAL) and its core is the Aneka container. The Aneka container is the building block of the middleware and represents the runtime environment for executing cloud applications. There are three classes of services in the container, viz. the fabric services which provide the access to the cloud resources, the execution services which are responsible for the scheduling and executing applications, and the foundation services which are the core management services in charge of metering applications, allocating resources, managing available nodes,

Fig. 2.2 Architecture of aneka cloud [17]

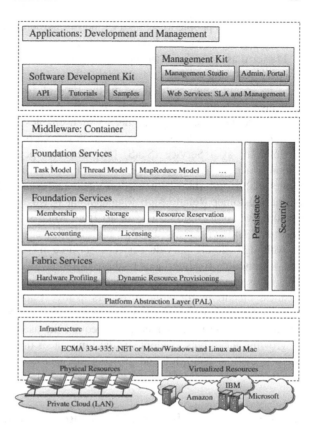

and keeping the services registry updated. In the application layer, Aneka provides a tool for managing the cloud, allowing administrators to easily start, stop, and deploy instances of the Aneka container on new resources and then reconfigure them dynamically to alter the behavior of the cloud. For more details about the Aneka cloud, please refer to [17, 75].

Corresponding to the different layers, clouds in general provide services at three different levels (IaaS, PaaS, and Saas [32]) as follows, although some providers can choose to expose services at more than one level.

Infrastructure as a Service (IaaS) [19] provisions hardware, software, and equipments (mostly at the unified resource layer, but can also include part of the fabric layer) to deliver software application environments with a resource usage-based pricing model. Infrastructure can scale up and down dynamically based on application resource needs. Typical examples are Amazon EC2 (Elastic Cloud Computing) Service (http://aws.amazon.com/ec2/) and S3 (Simple Storage Service) (http://aws.amazon.com/s3/) where compute and storage infrastructures are open to public access with a utility pricing model; Eucalyptus [61] is an open source Cloud implementation that provides a compatible interface to Amazon's

EC2, and allows people to set up a Cloud infrastructure at premise and experiment prior to buying commercial services.

Platform as a Service (PaaS) [17, 46] offers a high-level integrated environment to build, test, and deploy custom applications. General speaking, developers will need to accept some restrictions on the type of software that they can write in exchange for built-in application scalability. An example is Google's App Engine (http://code.google.com/appengine/), which enables users to build Web applications on the same scalable systems that power Google applications.

Software as a Service (SaaS) [58] delivers special-purpose software that is remotely accessible by consumers through the Internet with a usage-based pricing model. Salesforce (http://www.salesforce.com/) is an industry leader in providing online Customer Relationship Management (CRM) services. Live Mesh (http://explore.live.com/windows-live-mesh) from Microsoft allows files and folders to be shared and synchronised across multiple devices.

Although clouds provide services at three different levels (IaaS, PaaS, and Saas), standards for interfaces to these different levels still remain to be defined. This leads to interoperability problems between today's clouds, and there is little business incentives for cloud providers to invest additional resources in defining and implementing new interfaces. As clouds mature, and more sophisticated applications and services emerge that require the use of multiple clouds, there will be growing incentives to adopt standard interfaces that facilitate interoperability in order to capture emerging and growing markets in a saturated cloud market.

2.2 General Architecture of Cloud Workflow Systems

2.2.1 Cloud Workflow System Architecture

In this section, we will present a general architecture of a cloud workflow system. Obviously, as typical cloud software itself, the architecture of a cloud workflow system should be consistent to the general cloud software architecture. Therefore, as shown in Fig. 2.3, the general cloud workflow architecture can be a mapping of the general cloud system architecture.

Specifically, the application layer consists of cloud workflows (workflow applications for real-world business processes).

The platform layer is the cloud workflow system which provides a development and running platform for cloud workflows. All the system functionalities of a cloud workflow system such as workflow management, cloud resource management and QoS management are included. The application layer and the platform layer are usually self-maintained by the business organisation.[1]

---

[1] A cloud workflow system can be encapsulated as a platform service, i.e. PaaS (platform as a service). In such a case, the platform layer is maintained by external cloud service providers.

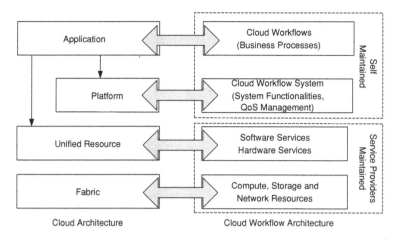

Fig. 2.3 Cloud workflow system architecture

The unified resource layer consists of both software services and hardware services that are required for the running of cloud workflows. Specifically, SaaS can provide massive number of software capabilities for processing different business tasks, while IaaS can provision on-demand and elastic computing power to meet the resource requirements for processing business tasks. In practice, software and hardware services can also be integrated together and encapsulated to be delivered as VMs (virtual machines).

The fabric layer is composed of low level hardware resources such as computing, storage and network resources. The unified layer and fabric layer are usually maintained by external cloud service providers.[2]

2.2.2 Example: Window Workflow Foundation Architecture

Here, as an example, we demonstrate the Windows Workflow Foundation (WWF, http://msdn.microsoft.com/en-us/netframework/aa663328) which is part of Microsoft.NET framework providing a foundation for developing workflow applications. Microsoft has developed the Windows Azure to help developers build, host and scale applications through Microsoft data centres. Windows Azure (http://www.microsoft.com/windowsazure/) is an operating system that serves as the development, service hosting, and service management environment for the Windows Azure platform. The Windows Azure platform consists of an infra-structure of hardware, software, network, and storage resources. Developers can

---

[2] The fabric layer can also be a virtual collection of local computing infrastructure (i.e. private cloud) and the commercial computing infrastructure (i.e. public cloud), i.e. hybrid cloud.

Fig. 2.4 Architecture of
WWF based cloud workflow
system

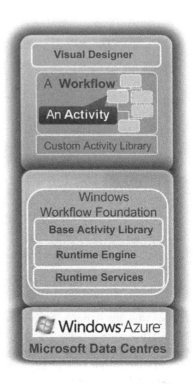

build and deploy applications as a hosted service for Windows Azure by using
the .NET Framework. Therefore, the Windows Azure platform is one of the ideal
hosting environment for WWF based workflow system.

Figure 2.4 depicts the architecture of a WWF based cloud workflow system.
The fabric and unified resource layers are built upon the Microsoft data centres
with Windows Azure, so that they can offer basic computing, storage and network
resource to the upper layers. The platform layer is WWF. WFF consists of three
main components, viz. base activity library, runtime engine, and runtime services.[3]
The base activity library contains frequently used workflow activities such as
assign, delay, invoke and so on. The runtime engine is the heart of WWF which
consists of the runtime classes and services required for the workflow execution.
The runtime services are responsible for such as scheduling activities, event
handling, exception, tracking and so on. At the application layer, the visual
designer provides customers a tool for flowchart-based workflow modelling with
activities such as if, sequence, pick, and parallel. In addition, customers can also
add custom-built activities into the customer activity library for use in the
workflow.

---

[3] A Developer's Introduction to Windows Workflow Foundation (WF) in .NET 4, http://
msdn.microsoft.com/en-us/library/ee342461.aspx.

Chapter 3
Cloud Workflow System Functionality

In this chapter, we will present the cloud workflow system functionality. In Sect. 3.1, we will first introduce the classical workflow reference model which defines the basic functionalities for a workflow system. In Sect. 3.2, we will then illustrate those system functionalities which are typical for the running of workflows in the cloud computing environment.

3.1 Classical Workflow Reference Model

Workflow system can be implemented for different purposes such as process management, process re-design/optimisation, system integration, achieving flexibility, and improving maintainability, and so on. Therefore, at the early stage of workflow systems, it is not clear what functionalities should be actually included in a workflow system. This confusion has not been solved until Workflow Management Coalition (WfMC) published its workflow reference model (http://www.wfmc.org/reference-model.html) in 1995. WfMC is an organisation which is dedicated to the standardisation of workflow management terminology and the standards for the exchange of data between workflow systems and applications. As shown in Fig. 3.1, the workflow reference model defines a workflow system and the most important system interfaces which enable products to interoperate at a variety of levels.

The workflow reference model defines 5 interfaces between the workflow enactment services and other 5 major components, viz. the process definition tools, the workflow client applications, the invoked applications, the other workflow enactment services, and the administration and monitoring tools, specifically, according to WfMC [82]:

X. Liu et al., *The Design of Cloud Workflow Systems*,
SpringerBriefs in Computer Science, DOI: 10.1007/978-1-4614-1933-4_3,

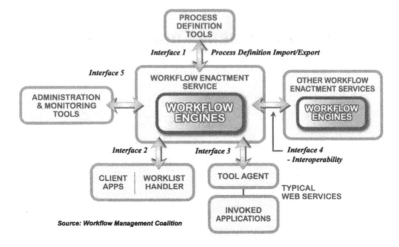

Fig. 3.1 WfMC's workflow reference model (http://www.wfmc.org/reference-model.html)

- Process Definition Tools Interface (1): definition of a standard interface between process definition and modelling tools and the workflow engine(s).
- Workflow Client Application Interface (2): definition of APIs for client applications to request services from the workflow engine to control the progression of processes, activities and work-items.
- Invoked Application Interface (3): a standard interface definition of APIs to allow the workflow engine to invoke a variety of applications, through common agent software.
- Workflow Interoperability Interface (4): definition of workflow interoperability models and the corresponding standards to support interworking.
- Administration & Monitoring Tools Interface (5): the definition of monitoring and control functions.

In the following, we will introduce the functionalities included in each component briefly. For more details, please refer to [2, 82].

Workflow enactment service and workflow engines: as shown in the reference model, workflow enactment service is the heart of a workflow system. A workflow enactment service can be a single workflow engine, or a collection of several workflow engines for the improvement of system scalability. A workflow engine provides those functionalities which are required for the completion of workflow instances. Specifically, the main functionalities of a workflow engine include: interpreting process definition models, generating new workflow instances, allocating correct resource for workflow activities, routing workflow instances, invoking applications, monitoring workflow execution, handling exceptions, and generating system logs. Clearly, workflow engines are the "core" of the workflow system. A workflow system may contain several workflow engines which are homogeneous. However, in order to complete some cross-domain workflows, it is possible to have some collaboration between several autonomous workflow systems which belong to different organisations. In this situation, several workflow enactment services can be linked together through interoperability (Interface 4).

Process definition tools: the process definitions tools are the set of components for creating, editing, and illustrating (also verification and analysis in some systems) workflow process definitions. Process definitions tools can adopt any visual modelling language such as Petri net [43] and Directed Acyclic Graph (DAG) [2] as the modelling language for workflow processes, which of course, should be interpretable by the workflow engines and support process definition import and export (Interface 1). Specifically, the main functionalities of a process definition tool include: generate process definitions, model the routing structures (such as sequence, parallelism, selection and iteration) with graphic components, define workflow activities (functional and non-functional requirements), and verify the correctness of workflow models (detect the semantic errors such as deadlock). Clearly, process definition tools are designed to realise most of the tasks in the workflow build-time stage.

Workflow client applications: the workflow client applications are the interfaces for the human resources (employees) who are involved in the workflow execution. The major part of a workflow client application is a worklist which contains the work items assigned to each employee by the workflow engine (Interface 2). Specifically, the main functionalities of a worklist handler include: list the work items assigned to a specific employee, provide necessary information about the work items, provide necessary state information about workflow execution, and report the progress of completing a work item (e.g. start, finish).

Invoked applications: besides human resources, execution of workflow activities often needs software applications. These software applications are invoked by workflow engines (Interface 3) when workflow activities are ready to start. Each invoked application is managed by a tool agent which is in charge of the communication between the workflow engine and the invoked application. The tool agent provides necessary activity information to the invoked application, and sends the execution results to the workflow engine. The invoked applications can be either the type of interactive applications which are triggered by the selection of a work item from the worklist and require the input from the employees (such as a spreadsheet or an electronic form), or the type of automatic applications which can be performed without user intervention (such as data processing programs). Meanwhile, these invoked applications can be either those software programs running in the local machines of an employee or those Web services running in the distributed servers.

Administration and monitoring tools: the administration and monitoring tools are in charge of the supervision and operational management of workflows (Interface 5). Specifically, the main functionalities of the administration and monitoring tools include: manage resource (both employees and software applications), configure system, inspect the workflow execution state, handle exceptions, record and report system performance, and many others. Clearly, the administration and monitoring tools not only include many runtime monitoring functionalities but also offline data analysis tasks which can be assisted by some data mining tools.

3.2 Basic Functionalities of Cloud Workflow Systems

3.2.1 Cloud Workflow System Functionality

Generally speaking, a cloud workflow system is the combination of workflow system and cloud services. The cloud workflow system itself can be regarded as a type of PaaS service since it can not only execute the cloud workflows as a type of software application but also provides the users with visual modelling tools to create their own workflow applications. Since visual modelling is actually a type of high level programming, a cloud workflow system can thus be regarded as a type of platform service. A cloud workflow system can be either running in private cloud of an organisation, or in public cloud where the underlying computing infrastructures are provided by the third party, or in a hybrid mode. In the hybrid mode, a cloud workflow system mainly relies on the resources in private cloud, and only uses public cloud for the scalability purpose. Meanwhile, in many cases, considering the security purpose, the cloud workflow system would store and manage the confidential data, and execute workflow instances which may need to access or produce these data in the private cloud, while execute others in public cloud. Therefore, a cloud workflow system should be able to employ and differentiate both private and public cloud services.

The workflow reference model suggested by WfMC defines the general components and interfaces of a workflow system. Therefore, instead of building from the scratch, we can design the basic system functionalities of a cloud workflow system by extending the workflow reference model with typical functionalities required for the integration of cloud services, such as cloud resource management and QoS management. The QoS management components will be further introduced in Chap. 4 given its critical importance in cloud workflow systems. Therefore, in this section, we will first present an overview of the system functionality, and then focus on the resource management components in a cloud workflow system.

As depicted in Fig. 3.2, the basic system functionalities of a cloud workflow system can be organised in the same way as the workflow reference model. Here, we only focus on several key components. In a cloud workflow system, the workflow modelling tool provides the system users an efficient way to create their workflow applications with the help of visual modelling components and/or scripting languages. Workflow specifications created by the users normally contain the information about the process structures, the activity definitions and the QoS requirements. The workflow enactment service is a collection of multiple parallel

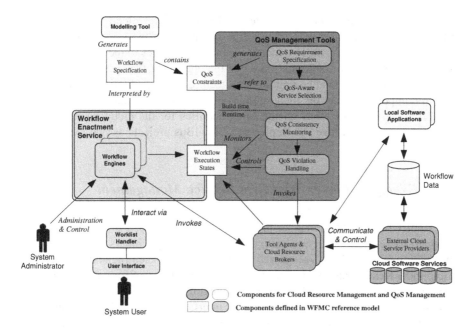

Fig. 3.2 System functionalities in cloud workflow system

workflow engines which are in charge of interpreting workflow specifications and coordinating all the management tools and necessary resources for workflow execution, such as the administration and control tools, worklist monitoring tools, workflow data and control flows, and software services. The workflow engines can invoke local software applications stored in the local repository (in the private cloud) and external cloud software services provided by the third party (in the public cloud). The workflow engines can search for cloud software services using the cloud resource brokers which perform the searching, reserving and auditing of cloud resources. After successful reservation of a cloud software service, a tool agent is created which is in charge of the communications with external cloud service providers, and the control of cloud software services according to the instructions received from the workflow engines.

Note that in cloud workflow systems, all the functional components are implemented as cloud services which are separated from the workflow engines. In such a case, the workflow engines, the functional components and other add-on tools can be hosted by different cloud infrastructure services. Based on the system workload, these components can be migrated or replicated to other resources, or request the provision of additional resources. For example, the workload (or bottleneck) on Web access for worklist or modelling tools can thus be offloaded to a different set of resources, rather than the same as the workflow engines. In addition, these components can work together as parts of the existing cloud workflow system, and they can also work as standalone cloud services for other applications or cloud workflow systems. Therefore, the cloud services based software components also contribute to the scalability of the whole system.

As mentioned in [62], the two most fundamental changes to the cloud workflow system compared with traditional ones are the change of the system architecture (the migration to the cloud computing architecture and the adoption of distributed system components), and the integration of cloud resources management tools. In the following, we will focus on the functionalities for the cloud resource management, and we will take the Kepler and CloudBus projects as two examples.

3.2.2 Example: Kepler Web/Grid Service Management

The Kepler project (https://kepler-project.org/), as introduced on its Website, 'is designed to help scientists, analysts, and computer programmers create, execute, and share models and analyses across a broad range of scientific and engineering disciplines. Kepler can operate on data stored in a variety of formats, locally and over the Internet, and is an effective environment for integrating disparate software components'. Using Kepler's graphical user interface, users simply select and then connect pertinent analytical components and data sources to create a "scientific workflow", an executable representation of the steps required to generate results. The Kepler software helps users share and reuse data, workflows, and components developed by the scientific community to address common needs. In Kepler, the workflow is viewed as a composition of independent components called *actors*. The communication between actors is through the interfaces called *ports*. Actors, or more precisely their ports, are connected to one another via *channels*. Although the actors are interconnected to each other, there are many possible execution semantics. Kepler uses an object called *director* to specify the execution semantics which defines how actors are executed and how they communicate with each other.

Kepler is designed for utilisation of Web/Grid services, not cloud services. The purpose of introducing the Web/Grid service management in Kepler here has two fold. First, regarding to software Web services, the management of Web services and SaaS cloud services are very similar. Second, since cloud workflow systems can be migrated from the existing grid workflow systems, we should take a look at the resource management tools in the grid environment, so that we can understand what can be inherited and what needs to be adapted.

As introduced in [55], one of the highlights of Kepler is the extension for Web services. Web services are becoming the standard means for accessing remote services in distributed systems. In Kepler, the WebService actor is in charge of the instantiation of Web services. Given the URL of a Web service description, the WebService actor can be instantiated to any particular operation specified in the service description. After instantiation, the WebService actor can be incorporated into a scientific workflow as if it were a local component. In particular, the WSDL-defined inputs and outputs of the service are made explicit via the instantiated actor's input and output ports. The extension to Grid services are realised by the Grid actors similarly to the WebService actors such as the GridFTP actor, GlobusJob actor and GlobusProxy actor.

3.2.3 Example: CloudBus Cloud Resource Management

The CloudBus project (http://www.cloudbus.org/cloudbus/) is a cloud computing platform for conducting fundamental research on the design and development for a range of market-oriented cloud applications such as cloud workflow systems. CloudBus is running in the Aneka cloud. Its ancestor is the GridBus project (http://www.gridbus.org/middleware/). Therefore, CloudBus is a typical example project as migration from grid to cloud. In general, the two basic ways to access cloud resources are through the user interface (e.g. resource management console in the form of Website or client tools) and the APIs. Aneka provides a set of APIs for the management of cloud resources. Specifically, Aneka exposes three SOAP Web services for service negotiation, reservation, and task submission. The negotiation and reservation services provide interfaces for negotiating resource use and reserving them in the Aneka cloud. The task Web service provides a SOAP interface which allows remote clients to submit jobs, monitor their status, and abort jobs. Cloud measurement tools are also required for the amount of data and computing power used, so that users are charged on the pay-as-you-go basis.

A key objective for the cloud resource management is the dynamic provision of cloud resources (scale up/down) according to real-time application requirements. CloudBus manages dynamic provisioning of compute and storage resources in the cloud with the help from tools and APIs provided by service providers. For instance, CloudBus can provision large number of VMs (virtual machines), such as the EC2 instances in the Amazon cloud, to meet the requirements for data and computation intensive workflow activities. Beside resource provision, the cloud workflow system also needs to implement workflow scheduling policies to optimise the task-to-resource assignment according to the QoS requirements. Given the cloud resource specification, and the specification for cloud workflows (including both functional and QoS requirements), CloudBus can direct a VM provisioning system to consolidate data centre loads by migrating VMs so that it could make scheduling decisions based on locality of data and compute resources. Meanwhile, for the persistent storage of workflow systems which stores and manages the metadata such as available resources, job queues, job status, and user data including large input and output files, CloudBus can facilitate different storage services such as Amazon S3, Google's BigTable, and the Windows Azure Storage Services.

Chapter 4
Cloud Workflow System Quality of Service

Along with system functionality, the management of quality of service (QoS) in cloud workflow system is attracting increasing and even more efforts [3, 31, 45, 47, 54, 73]. This is mainly because of the following two reasons. First, the cloud computing environment is very dynamic and uncertain. Therefore, it is difficult to achieve targeted service quality if without effective QoS management strategies; Second, cloud computing adopts the market-oriented model and strict service contracts. Therefore, high service quality is necessary for improving customer satisfaction and avoiding penalty for the breach of service contracts. Therefore, QoS management plays a significant role in cloud workflow systems, and hence included as significant part of this book. In Sect. 4.1, we will first present an overview about the QoS of Web and cloud services. In Sect. 4.2, we introduce the QoS of cloud workflows. In Sect. 4.3, a generic QoS framework is presented as a high level guideline for the design of software components to deliver lifecycle QoS support in cloud workflow systems. Afterwards, as concrete examples, specific strategies for performance management (on workflow response time), cost management (on data storage), reliability management (on data replication), and security management, will be discussed and demonstrated.

4.1 QoS of Cloud Services and Web Services

4.1.1 General QoS

In general, QoS refers to those non-functional requirements for Web services such as performance, reliability, availability and security and so on. For example, the response time for a Web search service should be less than 1 s, the availability of a Web file storage service should be higher than 99.99%. QoS management refers to a set of strategies dedicated to the delivery of targeted QoS requirements. Cloud services, as mentioned in Chap. 2, consist of three types of services, viz. SaaS,

X. Liu et al., *The Design of Cloud Workflow Systems*,
SpringerBriefs in Computer Science, DOI: 10.1007/978-1-4614-1933-4_4,
© The Author(s) 2012

PaaS and IaaS. Specifically, IaaS services are at the bottom layer which should be transparent to PaaS services, and PaaS services are at the middle layer which should be transparent to SaaS services. Clearly, the failures of the cloud services at the lower layer can lead to the failures at the higher layer(s). For example, if the reliability of the storage services (IaaS services) failed to achieve a targeted level (due to the failure rates of the hard disks), the cloud workflow systems (PaaS services) which are built upon these infrastructure services may also fail to achieve the targeted reliability, and so as the user business process applications (SaaS services). In addition, the QoS failures at a higher layer may be produced by much more factors than those at a lower layer. For example, the reliability failures of the business process applications can be caused by the problems of load balancing, version control, network, computation, and many others besides storage services. Therefore, for the same QoS dimensions such as performance and reliability, different measurements and corresponding strategies are required for different type of cloud services. Clearly, it is not practical for us to discuss all of them.

In this book, we basically focus on the QoS management in the cloud workflow systems from a platform service provider's point of view, i.e. how to ensure the satisfied QoS over the workflow lifecycle based on system management tools. Therefore, we assume that correct workflow applications are built and submitted by the users in the application layer and sufficient resources are available in the underlying infrastructure layer.

Here, we present a brief overview of some representative QoS dimensions for Web/Cloud services. More details can be found in [39].

- Cost: Cost, specifically referring to monetary cost here, is a very important QoS dimension for any software systems, especially in the commercial cloud computing environments where any usage of resources needs to be paid. In general, every other QoS dimensions such as performance, reliability and security all have a direct or indirect relationship to the cost in the sense that a significant increase of service quality normally means a sharp increase in the cost. Therefore, there are some researchers preferring not to include cost as a QoS dimension but rather as a general measurement or benchmark against all the QoS dimensions. In this book, we still treat cost as a typical QoS dimension like most of the researchers, and we will consider the affect of cost in the discussion with other QoS dimensions. Clearly, the trade-off between cost and other QoS dimensions always plays a core role in the design and implementation of QoS management strategies.
- Performance: Performance is a quality aspect of Web/Cloud service, which is measured in terms of throughput and response time. Higher throughput and short response time represent good performance of a Web/Cloud service. Throughput is measured by the number of requests that can be served during a specific period of time. Response time is the round-trip time between sending a request and receiving the response, e.g. the duration from submitting a workflow activity to receiving its execution result.

- Reliability: Reliability is the quality aspect of a Web/Cloud service that represents the degree of being capable of maintaining the service and service quality. The reliability of a Web/Cloud service can be measured by the number of failures such as service downtime and breach of service agreement over a specific period of time.
- Security: Security is the quality aspect of the Web/Cloud service of providing confidentiality and non-repudiation by authenticating the parties involved, encrypting messages, and providing access control. Security has added importance because Web service invocation occurs over the public Internet. The service provider can have different approaches and levels of providing security depending on the service requestor.
- Availability: Availability is the quality aspect of whether the Web/Cloud service is present or ready for immediate use. Availability can be measured by the probability that a service is available over a specific time.
- Integrity: Integrity is the quality aspect of how the Web/Cloud service maintains the correctness of the interaction in respect to the source. Proper execution of Web service transactions will provide the correctness of interaction. A transaction refers to a sequence of activities to be treated as a single unit of work. All the activities have to be completed to make the transaction successful. When a transaction does not complete, all the changes made are rolled back.
- Regulatory: Regulatory is the quality aspect of the Web service in conformance with the rules, the law, compliance with standards, and the established service level agreement. Web services use a lot of standards such as SOAP, UDDI, and WSDL. Strict conformance to correct versions of standards (for example, SOAP version 1.2) by service providers is necessary for proper invocation of Web services by service requestors.

4.1.2 SLA Management

In the cloud market, there are large numbers of similar or equivalent services provided by different parties. In order to make sure the successful delivery of paid services, service contract, as a formal document, is often negotiated and signed between the users and the service providers. A standard service contract may include many components such as the Header information (e.g. name, version, owner, responsibility assignment, and type), functional information (e.g. functional requirement, service operation, and invocation), and non-functional information (e.g. quality of service, transactions, service level agreement, semantics, and process) [29, 46]. Among them, SLA (service level agreement) formally defines the targeted/minimum level of services (service quality) that should be delivered by the service providers. In many cases, penalties may also be agreed upon in the case of non-compliance of SLA. Clearly, SLA management plays an important role in the fulfilment of service contracts. Specifically, the SLA lifecycle can have the following stages [29]:

- Identifying the provider. This stage is for searching and selecting a set of service providers through the use of cloud resources discovery or registry services.
- Defining the SLA. This stage is for identifying the specific terms to be included in the SLA. These terms are related to the QoS dimensions such as performance, reliability and security which must be monitored later on, and form the basis for penalty clauses.
- Agreeing on the terms of the SLA. This stage is for specifying the QoS constraints that must be met by the service provider during service provision and execution. Here, a negotiation process may be involved, and the penalty clauses may be specified.
- Provisioning and execution. This stage is for the service provision based on the agreed SLA which may include the interaction with the service provider's management services to setup the required resources.
- Monitoring SLA violations. This stage is for monitoring the specified SLA terms and ensuring that they are not being violated during the resource provision period.
- Destroying SLAs. This stage is for destroying the SLAs once the service provision has completed.
- Penalties for SLA violations. After the completion of a service provision, the monitoring data will be used to determine whether penalties need to be imposed on the service provider.

Clearly, in order to achieve satisfactory SLA management, a set of strategies are required to facilitate each stage in the SLA lifecycle, especially for stages 1, 3, 4 and 5, which play critical roles in the delivery of user expected service quality. Meanwhile, for different SLA terms (QoS dimensions), the ways for their specification, provision, and monitoring can be very different. Therefore, there are still many open questions for the SLA management for cloud services.

Here, we take Amazon's SLA management as an example to illustrate how it works in the commercial environment. Specifically, we take the SLA for Amazon EC2 (for computing) and S3 (for storage) services as representative examples. Here, we only focus on their SLA definitions and penalties. For more details, please refer to the respective links listed below.

EC2 SLA (http://aws.amazon.com/ec2-sla/): Amazon Elastic Compute Cloud (Amazon EC2) is a Web service that provides resizable compute capacity in the cloud. It is the major Amazon cloud service for provision computing resources. The official service commitment for EC2 SLA is quoted as "AWS will use commercially reasonable efforts to make Amazon EC2 available with an Annual Uptime Percentage of at least 99.95% during the Service Year". Here, "Annual Uptime Percentage" is calculated by subtracting from 100% the percentage of 5 min periods during the Service Year in which Amazon EC2 was in the state of "Region Unavailable." If the Annual Uptime Percentage for a customer drops below 99.95% for the Service Year, that customer is eligible to receive a Service Credit equal to 10% of the bill.

S3 SLA (http://aws.amazon.com/s3-sla/): Amazon Simple Storage Service (Amazon S3) provides a simple Web services interface that can be used to store and retrieve any amount of data, at any time, from anywhere on the web. It is the major Amazon cloud service for provision lasting storage resources. The official service commitment for S3 SLA is quoted as "AWS will use commercially reasonable efforts to make Amazon S3 available with a Monthly Uptime Percentage of at least 99.9% during any monthly billing cycle". Here, "Monthly Uptime Percentage" is calculated by subtracting from 100% the average of the Error Rates from each five minute period in the monthly billing cycle, where the error rate is calculated as the total number of internal server errors returned by Amazon S3 as error status "InternalError" or "ServiceUnavailable" divided by the total number of requests during a five-minute period. If the Monthly Uptime Percentage for a customer drops below 99.9%, that customer is eligible to receive a Service Credit equal to 10% of the bill (if the Monthly Uptime Percentage is equal to or greater than 99% but less than 99.9%), or 25% of the bill (if the Monthly Uptime Percentage is less than 99%).

4.2 QoS of Cloud/Grid Workflows

QoS management in cloud/grid workflow systems can be regarded as a representative and special scenario for the general QoS management in Web service based systems. It is representative for the reason that cloud/grid workflow systems are naturally distributed and composed of Web services, and cloud/grid workflows are modelled and built in a way of service composition. It is also special for the reason that QoS management for cloud/grid workflows not only applies to the service quality of individual services but also the collective quality of the workflow as a whole. Therefore, the measurement, monitoring and control strategies for workflow QoS share some similarities but have many unique features compared with their counterparts for individual services.

As summarised in [31, 39, 46, 87], the major dimensions for (grid) workflows are time, cost, reliability and security. Specifically, time is a basic measurement of performance, and it refers to the total time required for completing the workflow execution in a workflow system; cost refers to the cost associated with the execution of workflows including the cost for workflow management and the charge of the resource usage for processing workflow activities; and security refers to the confidentiality of the workflow execution and trustworthiness of resources. Clearly, the major workflow QoS dimensions are a subset of the general QoS dimensions for Web services. However, as mentioned above, the most different aspect lies in the collective behaviour of workflow applications. Here, for example, the overall completion time of a workflow consists of the individual durations for process every activity. But given the complex structure the software process, the overall completion is not a simple sum of the individual durations. A common case is that the completion time of a parallel workflow process is equal to the duration of the longest path, not the sum of all the activity durations. For another example, the reliability of a workflow depends on the reliability of all the service undertaken the execution of its workflow activities. The reliability of a single service is mainly related to the system failures which can be either caused by the hardware of software problems. However, the reliability of a workflow is not only affected by the system failures, but also the process failures which are caused by the business process exceptions [68, 69].

These differences will lead to significant changes in the QoS model which defines the QoS components and their relationships, and also the strategies for the estimation of QoS level, the specification of QoS constraints, the monitoring of QoS conformance, and the handling of QoS violations. Take the assignment of QoS constraints as example, there are two different ways. The first ways is to allow users to assign activity-level QoS constraints, and then the overall QoS can be assessed by computing the QoS constraints of all individual activities based on the specific QoS model. For example, a workflow reduction algorithm such as SWR(w) algorithm [20] can be employed to calculate the deadline for the entire workflow based on the desired execution time of individual workflow activities. The second way is to assign QoS constraints at workflow-level where users only define the overall workflow QoS requirements, and the workflow system will use automatic strategies to assign local and activity-level QoS constraints to the workflow segments and individual activities. For example, a deadline assignment approach such as Equal Slack and Equal Flexibility [41] can be applied to determine the expected execution time of individual activities based on the deadline for the entire workflow.

Similar to the lifecycle of a Web service, the cloud workflow also has its lifecycle. Here, we take a high level overview on the lifecycle of a typical workflow instance. Generally speaking, the lifecycle of a typical workflow instance consists of three major stages, viz. the modelling stage, the instantiation stage and the execution stage [2].

1) At the modelling stage, real world e-business or e-science processes are modelled or redesigned as cloud workflow specifications [27, 74] which may contain the process structures, task definitions for a number of workflow activities, and non-functional QoS requirements such as performance, reliability and security [71]. Based on the cloud workflow specifications, cloud workflow service providers will negotiate with their consumers to settle the service contracts which further determines such as objectives, prices and penalties.

2) At the instantiation stage, based on the service contracts, cloud workflow systems will search for candidate cloud software services which satisfy both functional and non-functional QoS requirements to fulfil the execution of workflow activities. After all the required software services are selected and reserved, cloud workflow instances are ready for execution.

3) At the execution stage, cloud workflow execution engines will coordinate the data and control flows according to the workflow specifications obtained at

the modelling stage and employ the candidate software services reserved at the instantiation stage to execute all the workflow activities. Besides, in dynamic system environments, necessary workflow runtime management such as monitoring and exception handling mechanisms will ensure the detection and recovery of functional and QoS violations so that service contracts can be successfully fulfilled.

Given the above description, it is evident that satisfactory QoS cannot be achieved missing the efforts in any of the stages. Therefore, lifecycle QoS management is essential in cloud workflow systems.

4.3 A Generic QoS Framework

There are a number of existing studies and projects investigating the support of specific QoS requirements in different software systems. However, due to the large differences between these QoS dimensions by nature, conventional software systems often adopt different sets of software components for different QoS dimensions. Therefore, when a new QoS dimension needs to be supported by the system, a set of new software components need to be developed and run independently. However, if there is no unified framework to guide the design and development process, the system complexity as well as the software development cost can be rapidly on the rise. Therefore, start from the design of a cloud workflow system, a generic framework is required to integrate and manage the software components for the support of different QoS dimensions. In this book, we do not intend to cover the detailed strategies for all QoS dimensions, which is neither possible nor necessary. Instead, our focus is a generic framework which can facilitate the support of different QoS dimensions in cloud workflow systems. Meanwhile, in a cloud workflow system, a workflow instance needs to undergo several stages before its completion, specifically, the modelling stage, the instantiation stage and the execution stage. Evidently, satisfactory QoS cannot be achieved with the sole effort in any single stage, but an effective lifecycle QoS support. To this end, the capabilities of generic software components which are required to realise lifecycle QoS support for cloud workflow applications should be identified in the first place. After that, strategies and algorithms for specific QoS requirements can be designed, implemented and managed by the generic framework as a vehicle for workflow QoS management.

In this section, we present a generic QoS framework for lifecycle QoS support in cloud workflow systems.

Our generic QoS framework is depicted in Fig. 4.1. Based on the three major stages of a workflow instance lifecycle, the framework consists of four components as shown in the outer cycle of Fig. 4.1, viz. QoS requirement specification, QoS-aware service selection, QoS consistency monitoring and QoS violation handling, which are implemented in a consecutive order to provide lifecycle QoS support for

Fig. 4.1 A generic QoS
framework

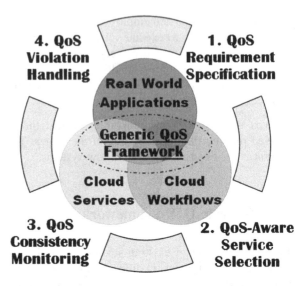

cloud workflow instances. The three inner cycles stand for the important factors involved in the design and application of cloud workflow systems, viz. real world applications, cloud workflows and cloud services. All the basic requirements for cloud workflows come from real world applications (e.g. business and scientific processes). Real world applications need to be abstracted by workflow service consumers with the support of workflow modelling tools and then create cloud workflow specifications. After these specifications are submitted to the cloud workflow engines, instances of these cloud workflow specifications, or cloud workflow instances for short, are executed with the underlying cloud services such as software and infrastructure services, which are normally with very dynamic service quality.

1) *QoS requirement specification*. The first component of our generic framework is QoS requirement specification at the modelling stage. The specification of QoS requirements is a very important part of the whole workflow specification which may consist of process structures, task definitions, functional and non-functional (QoS) requirements. In general, QoS requirements can be specified in the form of either quantitative or qualitative QoS constraints.

An entire workflow instance is made of many individual workflow activities. Accordingly, there are both workflow-level QoS constraints (coarse-grained QoS constraints) and activity-level constraints (fine-grained QoS constraints). In practice, cloud workflow service consumers usually only prefer to assign a few coarse-grained QoS constraints, e.g. one deadline and several milestones for the requirement on workflow response time. However, for service selection and monitoring purposes, fine-grained QoS constraints for individual workflow activities are necessary. Therefore, specific approaches are required to propagate a number of fine-grained constraints based on several consumer specified coarse-grained ones. Note that most coarse-grained constraints and fine-grained constraints are not in a simple linear accumulation relationship (except cost), i.e. the sum of fine-grained constraints for a group of workflow activities is not equal to their coarse-grained constraint. For example, the deadline for a workflow segment only applies to the completion time of the last workflow activities in workflow segment, while the sum of the execution time for all the workflow activities can be much larger than the deadline, especially when there are many parallel paths in the workflow process. Therefore, sophisticated setting approaches need to be designed to address the propagation of fine-grained constraints for different QoS requirements, and ensure the consistency between the coarse-grained and fine-grained constraints. Here, the consistency means that if every individual workflow activities can satisfy its fine-grained QoS constraint, then the whole coarse-grained QoS constraint can be satisfied, and vice versa.

Furthermore, since at the workflow modelling stage, the execution states of workflow instances at runtime are uncertain such as which execution path is taken in a choice structure and which execution path takes the longest execution time in a parallel structure. Meanwhile, the quality of the available cloud service is also uncertain. Therefore, some probabilistic and forecasting strategies are also required to facilitate setting of QoS constraints.

2) *QoS-aware service selection*. The second component of our generic framework is the QoS-aware service selection at the instantiation stage. Given the task definition and functional requirement for each workflow activity, cloud workflow systems can usually search for and obtain many available software services in the cloud. However, these software services will be further selected based on non-functional requirements, specifically, the fine-grained QoS constraints assigned for each task by the first component. Clearly, only those software services which have higher quality then the QoS constraints can be selected by this service selection component.

Since there may be more than one QoS dimensions, the selected software services should be able to satisfy all of them. But sometimes, if this is not possible, some trade-off could be made but in a best-effort way to meet most of them. Therefore, some ranking functions should be designed to evaluate and rank the available software services. Furthermore, given some QoS requirements such as reliability and availability, the component will probably select multiple software services from different service providers at this stage to ensure there is some redundancy, namely backup services, to handle the discrepancy during runtime workflow execution. Clearly, redundancy incurs extra cost. Therefore, at this stage, only one primary software service (e.g. the one with the highest rank) will be selected and reserved. As for other backup services, the component will only keep their information without actual reservation. However, some service providers such as Amazon provide discounted prices for reserved services (e.g. Amazon EC2 Reserved Instances or Spot Instances, http://aws.amazon.com/ec2/), hence it is also possible to book for some reserved services in advance

3) *QoS consistency monitoring*. The third component in our generic framework is QoS consistency monitoring at the execution stage. QoS consistency monitoring

starts from the very beginning of cloud workflow execution. Here, QoS consistency means that the real service quality at the execution stage is consistent with the QoS constraints assigned at the modelling stage. Due to the dynamic nature of cloud computing, workflow execution state needs to be kept under constant monitoring and QoS verification. Here, QoS verification is to check the workflow execution state against QoS constraints.

The verification for the quality of a single service is very intuitive, i.e. a simple comparison between QoS constraint and the runtime quality measurement. However, the problem becomes non-trivial for monitoring large-scale cloud workflow instances. First, in order to monitor, i.e. conduct QoS verification at anytime of the execution of a large-scale workflow instance, some probabilistic and forecasting strategies are required to estimate the quality of software services for those non-commenced workflow tasks. This is very similar to QoS constraint setting in the first component but with the access to runtime information. Second, the most intuitive way to conduct QoS verification is to check QoS consistency at every workflow task, so that if every individual software service satisfies its QoS constraint, the quality of the entire workflow instance can be achieved. Clearly, this is very inefficient and probably results in a rapid increase on the cost for QoS management. However, if we have the runtime information or knowledge that some of the software services are of very stable quality (such as produced by very reputable service providers, or having very satisfactory records for the latest several workflow instances), the QoS verification can usually be skipped safely. Therefore, we can choose to conduct QoS verification only at some selected activity points, which can be named as QoS checkpoints, to save the cost. However, different QoS dimensions will probably require different information and have different rules for selecting QoS checkpoints. The selection results for different QoS dimensions will need to be compared and compromised in order to make efficient and effective selection.

4) *QoS violation handling*. The last component of our generic framework is QoS violation handling at the execution stage. When the violation of QoS constraint is detected by the monitoring component, some recovery actions should be taken to handle and try to bring the workflow execution state back to consistency. QoS violation handing is very different from the conventional exception handling of software functional failures in traditional software systems. For example, in traditional software systems, when functional failures happen, the system state can be rolled back to its last checkpoint and restart the execution. Such a rollback-and-restart process can be repeated until functional failures are solved. However, as for non-functional QoS violations, this general strategy is often useless. For example, if temporal violations are detected, i.e. there are some execution delays, the rollback-and-restart strategy cannot compensate for the delays but may make the situation even worse. Actually, the time delays can only be compensated by the subsequent non-commenced workflow tasks. If we can reduce the execution time of the subsequent workflow tasks by such as recruiting additional resources or workflow rescheduling (by allocating the activities to fast resources or reducing their queuing time). In such a case, the existing time delays can be compensated

and the workflow execution state can be brought back to consistency. Meanwhile, for other QoS requirements such as reliability and security, if violations have been detected at the current checkpoint, the handling process is to minimise the loss while take proactive actions to prevent these violations from happening again in the future.

Generally speaking, for QoS violation handing, firstly, we should try to mini-mise the existing loss, and secondly (or actually more importantly), we should prevent these violations in the subsequent workflow as much as possible.

Based on the generic QoS framework as a high level guideline, in the following four sections, we will present concrete examples on the time management (on temporal constraints), cost management (on data storage), reliability management (on data replication), and security management (on privacy). Note that due to the on-going research progress, not every QoS dimension except performance man-agement has covered the four components of the generic QoS framework intro-duced above. Therefore, the works presented next are not strictly organised according to the sequence of the workflow lifecycle but may focus on the current main contributions for a specific component.

4.4 Example 1: Time Management (on Temporal Constraints)

The time (or performance) framework focuses on the workflow performance, or more specifically, it focuses on the response time of workflow applications. By following our generic QoS framework, the performance framework consists of four components which can provide a lifecycle support for high performance in cloud workflow systems.

1) *Temporal constraint setting*. The first component is temporal constraint setting which assigns both coarse-grained temporal constraints and fine-grained temporal constraints in cloud workflow specifications at the modelling stage. The setting of high quality temporal constraints is very important to the successful on-time completion of cloud workflows.

In our performance framework, temporal constraint setting is realised through a three-step process. The first step is a forecasting process where the workflow activity duration intervals are predicted by a time-series forecasting strategy. The second step is a win–win negotiation process between service consumers and service providers to specify the coarse-grained temporal constraints. The third step is a propagation process where fine-grained temporal constraints are set auto-matically based on the results of the second step.

The detailed strategy and algorithms for the temporal constraint setting com-ponent can be found in [49].

2) *Temporal-aware service selection*. The second component is temporal-aware service selection which selects and reserves suitable cloud software services for individual workflow tasks. For temporal constraints alone, the service selection will probably only consider the processing power of the software services such as

the speed of the CPU units and the size of the memory spaces. However, in the real world, the service selection process often needs to consider other QoS constraints such as reliability and security. All these QoS constraints serve as critical criteria for the selection of cloud services and resource management in cloud workflow systems [29].

3) *Temporal consistency monitoring*. The third component is temporal consistency monitoring. Based on a temporal consistency model, the temporal consistency states of cloud workflows should be under constant monitoring in order to detect potential temporal violations in a timely fashion. However, as mentioned in our generic framework, the accumulated cost for temporal verification can be huge in large-scale cloud workflow instances. Therefore, cost-effective strategies need to be designed to detect potential temporal violations in an efficient fashion.

In our performance framework, the function of temporal consistency state monitoring is realised through a two-step process. The first step is temporal checkpoint selection. Given the probability based temporal consistency model, our minimum probability time redundancy based checkpoint selection strategy can choose the minimal set of activity points (i.e. necessary and sufficient checkpoints) for temporal verification. Here, necessity means that only those activity points where real temporal inconsistency states take place are selected and sufficiency means that there are no any omitted activity points. The second process is temporal verification which checks the current temporal consistency states at selected checkpoints with our probability based temporal consistency model. In our performance framework, only two types of temporal consistency states (viz. recoverable and non-recoverable) are defined [48]. Accordingly, only one type of temporal checkpoint and one time of temporal verification are required to determine the current temporal consistency state.

The detailed strategy and algorithms for the temporal consistency monitoring can be found in [53]. In Appendix A, a temporal checkpoint selection and verification strategy is presented.

4) *Temporal violation handling*. The last component is temporal violation handling which deals with recovery of temporal violations. Based on the results of the previous component for monitoring temporal consistency, a necessary and sufficient checkpoint is selected which means a potential temporal violation is detected. When a temporal violation is detected, temporal violation handling strategies should be executed. In our performance framework, we mainly focus on those statistically recoverable temporal violations [51] which can be recovered by light-weight temporal violation handling strategies. For such a purpose, representative metaheuristics based workflow rescheduling strategies are investigated, adapted and implemented under a novel general two-stage local workflow rescheduling strategy to handle temporal violations. Since our temporal violation handling strategy is fully automatic and only utilises existing system resources without recruiting additional ones, the cost of temporal violation handling can be significantly reduced compared with conventional heavy-weight temporal violation handling strategies.

In our performance framework, we have defined three levels of recoverable temporal violations, viz. level I, level, II and level III violations, and designed their corresponding handling strategies, viz. TDA (time deficit allocation), ACOWR (ant colony optimisation based two-stage local workflow rescheduling strategy) and TDA + ACOWR (the combined strategy of TDA and ACOWR). ACOWR is the major strategy which attempts to compensate for the time deficits with the reduced workflow execution time through optimising the workflow scheduling plan. Here, "two-stage" means a two-stage searching process designed in our strategy to strike a balance between time deficit compensation and the completion time of other activities while "local" means the rescheduling of "local" workflow segments with "local" resources. Our temporal violation handling strategy only utilises existing resources which are currently deployed in the system instead of recruiting additional resources. Meanwhile, unlike global rescheduling which modifies the global task-resource list for the entire workflow instance, our strategy only focuses on the local workflow segment and optimises the integrated task-resource list.

The detailed strategy and algorithms for the temporal violation handling component can be found in [51]. In Appendix A, a novel general two-stage local workflow rescheduling strategy is presented.

4.5 Example 2: Cost Management (on Data Storage)

Cloud computing systems offer a new way for deploying large-scale data and computation intensive applications. As IaaS (Infrastructure as a Service) is a very popular way to deliver computing resources in the cloud [67], the heterogeneity of computing systems [92] of one service provider can be well shielded by virtualisation technology. Hence, users can deploy their applications in unified resources without any infrastructure investment, where excessive processing power and storage can be obtained from commercial cloud service providers. With the pay-as-you-go model, the total application cost in the cloud highly depends on the strategy of storing the application datasets, e.g. storing all the generated application datasets in the cloud may result in a high storage cost since some datasets may be seldom used but large in size; in contrast, if we delete all the generated datasets and regenerate them every time when needed, the computation cost may be very high too.

A good strategy is to find a balance to selectively store some popular datasets and regenerate the rest when needed [88]. However, sometimes users may have certain preferences on storing some particular datasets due to various reasons, e.g. guaranteeing immediate access to certain datasets. Storage of this kind of datasets is not only dependent on their cost, and sometimes is beyond system's control. Furthermore, because of the scalability and the dynamic provisioning mechanism of the cloud computing system, the application cost in the cloud would change from time to time whenever new datasets are generated or the datasets' usage frequencies are changed. The cloud service provider should be able to provide benchmarking services to users, who often wish to know the minimum cost of running their applications in the cloud.

In this section, we discuss the QoS of cost-effective datasets storage in the cloud. Based on a Data Dependency Graph (DDG), we address the issue of computation and storage trade-off in the cloud. In terms of constrains setting, users' investment budgets form the maximum constrains for the datasets storage. In terms of QoS aware service selection, we present a minimum cost benchmarking approach which can find the best trade-off of computation and storage in the cloud. This minimum cost benchmark can be used to evaluate the cost-effectiveness of different data storage services for selection. Furthermore, we develop some cost-effective storage strategies with the pay-as-you-go model in the cloud, which can be either delivered as services for users or substituted the old service when cost violations occur.

4.5.1 Cost Model of Datasets Storage in the Cloud

4.5.1.1 Data Dependency Graph

Application datasets in the cloud often have dependencies, i.e. computation task can operate on one or more datasets and generate new one(s). Data provenance is a kind of important metadata in which the dependencies between datasets are recorded [72]. Hence we create a Data Dependency Graph (DDG) [90] based on data provenance, which records the generation relationship of all the datasets (Fig. 4.2).

DDG is a directed acyclic graph (DAG). This is because DDG records the provenances of how datasets are derived in the system as time goes on. In another word, it depicts the generation relationships of datasets. When some of the deleted intermediate datasets need to be reused, we do not need to regenerate them from the original input data. With DDG, the system can find the predecessors of the demanding dataset, so they can be regenerated from their nearest stored predecessors.

4.5.1.2 Cost Rate of Datasets Storage in the Cloud

As indicated earlier, in a commercial cloud computing environment, if the users want to deploy and run applications, they need to pay for the resources used. The resources are offered by cloud service providers, who have their cost models to charge the users. In general, there are two basic types of resources in the cloud: storage and computation. Popular cloud services providers' cost models are based on these types of resources. For example, Amazon cloud services' prices are as follows:

Fig. 4.2 A simple data
dependency graph (DDG)

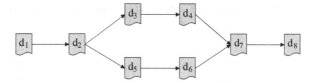

$0.15 per Gigabyte per month for the storage resources;
$0.1 per CPU instance hour for the computation resources.

In this book, we define our datasets storage cost model in cloud computing
system as follows:

$$Cost = C + S,$$

where the total cost of the system, *Cost*, is the sum of *C*, which is the total cost of
computation resources used to regenerate datasets, and *S*, which is the total cost of
storage resources used to store the datasets.

To utilise the datasets storage cost model, we define the attributes for the
datasets which can be found in our work. Briefly, for a dataset d_i, it has a cost rate
(***CostR***), which means the average cost per time unit of dataset d_i in the system.
The value $CostR_i$ depends on the storage status of d_i, where

$$CostR_i = \begin{cases} StorageCostRate, & d_i = stored \\ GenerationCost * UsageFrequency, & d_i = deleted \end{cases}$$

Hence, the total cost rate of storing a DDG is the sum of *CostR* of all the
datasets in it which is $\sum_{d_i \in DDG} CostR_i$. Given a time duration, the total cost of
storing a DDG is the integral of the cost rate in this duration as a function of time t,
which is

$$Total\_Cost = \int_t \left(\sum_{d_i \in DDG} CostR_i \right) \cdot dt$$

We further define the storage strategy of a DDG as *S*, where $S \subseteq DDG$, which
means storing the datasets in *S* in the cloud and deleting the rest. We denote the
cost rate of storing a DDG with the storage strategy *S* as *SCR*, where

$$SCR = \left(\sum_{d_i \in DDG} CostR_i \right)_S$$

Based on the definition above, the system's cost rate highly depends on the
storage strategy of the datasets. Storing different datasets will lead to different
cost rates for the system. Our target is to find the minimum cost of datasets
storage for users as benchmark and also offering users cost-effective storage
strategies, with which users can verify and satisfy the cost constraints of their
applications.

4.5.2 Minimum Cost Benchmarking of Datasets Storage in the Cloud

Due to the pay-as-you-go model, cost-effectiveness becomes an extremely important factor for the data storage strategy of scientific applications in the cloud. As increasing number of datasets is generated and stored in the cloud, users need to evaluate the cost effectiveness of their storage strategies. Hence the cloud service providers should be able and need to provide benchmarking services that can inform the minimum cost of storing the application datasets in the cloud. As we discussed earlier, there is a trade-off between computation and storage in the cloud. The benchmarking algorithms are to find this trade-off, which form the minimum cost storage strategy for scientific applications in the cloud.

Finding the minimum cost storage strategy is a difficult problem because there is a large number of datasets having complex dependencies with each other in the cloud. To solve this problem, we present a novel CTT-SP (Cost Transitive Tournament-Shortest Path) algorithm which has three major steps.

1) We construct a Cost Transitive Tournament (CTT) based on the DDG, where all the paths from the start dataset to the end datasets have a one-to-one mapping to the storage strategies of the DDG.
2) We set weights to the edges in the CTT which makes the length of the paths equivalent to the cost rates of the corresponding storage strategies.
3) We can use the well-known Dijkstra algorithm to find the Shortest Path (SP) in the CTT, which represents the minimum cost storage strategy of the DDG.

Figure 4.3 shows an example of the CTT-SP algorithm in a linear DDG with three datasets and the pseudo code of the algorithm can be found in Appendix B.

For a general DDG, the CTT-SP algorithm can be extended to a recursive algorithm which is polynomial with the worst case time complexity of $O(n^9)$ [90]. The CTT-SP algorithm can be used as an on-demand minimum cost benchmarking approach for datasets storage in the cloud. Whenever users want to know the minimum cost of storing the dataset, the general CTT-SP algorithm can be called to calculate the minimum cost benchmark for users.

4.5.3 Cost-Effective Datasets Storage Strategies

In a commercial cloud computing environment, theoretically, the system can offer unlimited storage resources. All the datasets generated by the applications can be stored, if the users are willing to pay for the required resources. Hence, for applications in the cloud, whether to store the datasets or not is not an easy decision anymore. The datasets vary in size, and have different generation costs and usage frequencies. Some of them may be used frequently whilst some others may be not. On one hand, it is most likely not cost effective to store all these

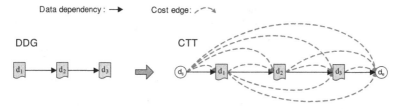

Fig. 4.3   An example of the CTT-SP Algorithm with three datasets

datasets in the cloud. On the other hand, if we delete them all, regeneration of frequently used datasets would normally impose a high computation cost. Meanwhile, the storage strategy should also consider the users' tolerance of data accessing delay. Based on the factors above, we develop two storage strategies as follows which are able to satisfy the application cost constraints as well as the time constraints of data accessing delay.

4.5.3.1 Cost Rate Based Strategy

In this strategy, we compare generation cost rate and storage cost rate for every dataset to decide its storage status [88]. The strategy can guarantee that the stored datasets in the system are all necessary, and can dynamically check whether the regenerated datasets need to be stored, and if so, adjust the storage strategy accordingly.

Furthermore, we introduce a parameter to this strategy that reflects users' tolerance of data accessing delay [91]. By flexibly adjusting the parameter, datasets with higher storage cost may be storage according to users' preferences.

This strategy contains three algorithms dealing with the following three situations:

1) new datasets are generated in the system;
2) the existing datasets' usage frequencies are changed;
3) the deleted datasets are regenerated. The pseudo codes of the algorithms can be found in Appendix B.

By only comparing generation cost rate and storage cost rate of the dataset itself to decide its storage status, this strategy is highly efficient and scalable.

4.5.3.2 Local-Optimisation Based Strategy

In this strategy, we partially utilise the CTT-SP algorithm, which can find the minimum cost storage strategy of a linear DDG [88]. We partition the general DDG to small linear segments and utilise the CTT-SP algorithm to achieve the localised optimal. Furthermore, in order to satisfy the time constraints of datasets'

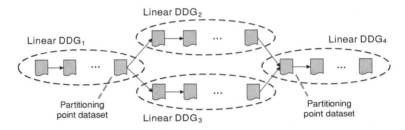

Fig. 4.4 An example of DDG partitioning

regeneration, we set rules to delete the over-length cost-edges in the CTT graph, which guarantees all the found storage strategies can satisfy users' tolerance of data accessing delay. The improved CTT-SP algorithm can be found in Appendix B and the strategy contains the following rules:

1) Given a general DDG, the datasets to be stored first are the ones that users have no tolerance of accessing delay on them. This is to guarantee the immediate availability when these datasets are needed.

2) Then, the DDG is partitioned into separate sub DDGs by the stored datasets. For every sub DDG, if it is a linear one, we use the improved CTT-SP algorithm to find its storage strategy; otherwise, we find the datasets that have multiple direct predecessors or successors, and use these datasets as the partitioning points to divide it into sub linear DDGs, as shown in Fig. 4.4. Then we use the improved linear CTT-SP algorithm to find their storage strategies. This is the essence of local optimisation.

3) When new datasets are generated in the system, they will be treated as a new sub DDG and added to the old DDG. Correspondingly, its storage status will be calculated in the same way as the old DDG.

4) When a dataset's usage frequency is changed, we will re-calculate the storage status of the sub linear DDG that contains this dataset.

By utilising the CTT-SP algorithm, this strategy is highly cost-effective with reasonable runtime computation complexity.

4.6 Example 3: Reliability Management (on Data Replication)

In this section we discuss about the QoS management of data reliability in cloud workflow systems. The data reliability management has become a very important issue due to the development of storage services in current commercial cloud computing systems. The goal of reliability management is to achieve the service reliability constraints by data replication while, at the same time, the cost for meeting this demand need to be minimised. In terms of QoS requirement specification, various data reliability requirements form the lower constraints of the data reliability management. In terms of QoS-aware service selection, we present an incremental replication approach in which the data replication services and the time point calculating services are activated at certain time points. The consistency monitoring of the data replicas can be achieved by proactive scanning of all the data, and the incremental replication approach is reactivated when violation occurs, i.e. the reliability requirement is not met.

4.6.1 Data Replication

The cloud workflow system is able to cooperate many applications and systems in the Cloud, which include many data-intensive applications such as scientific cloud workflow applications [40, 91] and large-scale data storage systems [14, 35, 80], etc. Therefore, the reliability management for large-scale data has played a very important role in cloud workflow systems. This section mainly focuses on the data replication area, which provides data reliability assurance by creating replicas.

At the software layer, modern distributed computing systems generally use data replication technology to prevent data loss from hardware failure for supporting data reliability. For data reliability purposes, current cloud data storage systems such as Amazon S3 storage service (http://aws.amazon.com/s3/), Google File System [35] and Hadoop Distributed File System [14] store three replicas by default. However, such typical three-replica reliability strategy may not be applicable to workflow systems in the cloud. For example, scientific cloud workflow applications usually contain a large number of tasks. During the execution, large volumes of intermediate data are generated and the amount of them could be much larger than the size of the original input. However, some intermediate data are only aimed for temporary use. For example, in the pulsar searching workflow application presented in [91], all the intermediate data are deleted after having been used, or in the future some of these intermediate data will be stored for later use but it is uncertain for how long the data need to be stored. For the storage of such large amount and temporarily used data, typical three-replica reliability strategy may cause huge resource waste, which would significantly affect the cost effectiveness of the workflow system. With the pay-as-you-go model, it is believed that these additional costs are finally passed on to the users.

In this section, we describe the data storage reliability model and a novel cost-effective dynamic data replication strategy which is mainly designed for the data reliability issue of workflow systems in the cloud. By applying the reliability model and the replication strategy, the storage cost for intermediate data in the workflow system can be greatly reduced, and the cost-effectiveness data replication management goal can be reached.

4.6.2 Data Storage Reliability Model

For the data reliability issue of workflow systems in the cloud, we need to build a reliability model first. In a cloud computing environment, all the storage and computing processes are conducted in data centres. Data centres contain large amount of commodity computing and storage units. These storage units all have certain life spans, and the probability of storage hardware failure or data loss increases according to storage duration. In classical theories [66, 86], the relationship between failure rate and storage duration follows the exponential distribution with failure rate λ, which equals to the expected number of failures of a storage unit in a certain time: $Reliability = 1 - F(x) = e^{-\lambda T}$, where $F(x)$ is an exponential cumulative distribution function. Based on this storage exponential distribution theory, our data storage reliability model is proposed.

Assume that the number of storage units be m. Based on the storage exponential distribution theory, the reliability assurance of all m storage units can be described by a failure rate set $FRS = \{\lambda_1, \lambda_2, \lambda_3, \ldots \lambda_m\}$ Assume that X be the lower bound of the reliability requirement constraint which is requested by the user. Thus the data storage reliability model demonstrating the relationship between the lower reliability bound X, the number of replicas and the storage duration can be expressed as the equation below:

$$X = 1 - \prod_{i=1}^{k} \left(1 - e^{-\lambda_i T_k}\right) \tag{4.1}$$

In this equation, k is the number of replicas, and T_K is the longest storage duration. The right-hand side of this equation describes the probability that no failure happens during the storage duration of T_K when k data replicas are stored in storage units with failure rates $\lambda_1, \lambda_2, \lambda_3, \ldots \lambda_m$ respectively. By using this equation, our aim is to derive T_K, which indicates the storage duration that k replicas can assure the reliability requirement X.

This reliability model can be applied to many different situations to meet various kinds of reliability requirement constraints. However, as most modern large-scale storage systems store three replicas by default, in this section, we only illustrate the situation that the number of replicas is no more than 3.

We conduct simplification on Eq. (4.1) for the purpose of calculation. After the simplification of the equation, we obtain three functions as follows:

$$\text{When k = 1, } F(T_1) = e^{-\lambda_1 T_1}\big/X \tag{4.2}$$

$$\text{When k = 2, } F(T_2) = Xa^{\lambda_1 + \lambda_2} - a^{-\lambda_1} - a^{-\lambda_2} + 1, \text{where } a = e^{(T_2)} \tag{4.3}$$

$$\text{When k = 3, } F(T_3) = Xb^{(\lambda_1+\lambda_2+\lambda_3)} - b^{(\lambda_1+\lambda_2)} - b^{(\lambda_1+\lambda_3)} - b^{(\lambda_2+\lambda_3)} + b^{(\lambda_1)}$$
$$+ b^{(\lambda_2)} + b^{(\lambda_3)} - 1, \text{ where } b = e^{(T_3)} \tag{4.4}$$

4.6.3 Cost-Effective Incremental Replication Strategy

Based on the reliability model and functions above, the dynamic data replication strategy named Cost-effective Incremental Replication (CIR) is proposed.

The idea of CIR is to use the minimum number of replicas while meeting the data reliability requirement constraint. Due to the uncertainty of the data storage durations, it needs to decide how many replicas are sufficient to meet the reliability requirement. Initially, the minimum data replica number is bound to 1 by default, i.e. only the original data will be stored and no extra replicas will be made at the beginning of a data storage instance. When time goes by, more replicas need to be incrementally created at certain time points to maintain the reliability assurance. Based on the reliability model in Sect. 4.6.2, by solving reliability functions (4.2), (4.3) and (4.4) separately, the time points for replica creation can be determined, which indicate when the current number of replicas cannot assure the data reliability requirement any longer and a new replica should be created. At the beginning of each data storage instance or when the latest replica creation time point reaches, a process maintained by the storage system for calculating the replica creation time points is activated.

The pseudo code of CIR is in Appendix C.

4.7 Example 4: Security Management (on Privacy)

Security plays an important role in distributed computing systems [25]. To ensure the high QoS of cloud workflow systems, we focus on the security problems brought by different types of components, large volume of heterogeneous data, and unpredictable execution processes. Since some general aspects of system security such as service quality and data security are partially included in the previous performance and data management components, this section emphasises the trust management which plays an important role in the security management [76] of cloud workflow system QoS. In the large scale workflow applications, to match high requirements of quality and scalability, an efficient and adaptive trust management is an indispensable part of the cloud workflow system platform [13, 81]. On the basis of trust management, the privacy protection could be considered to enhance the whole security management in cloud workflow systems under the risk of cloud environments to enhance users' confidence. Besides, user management is essential to guarantee system security and avoid illegal access. Facing the complex network structures in the cloud environment, we also need encryption technology to protect privacy, integrity, authenticity and undeniableness. Clearly, security management in cloud workflow systems is quite broad to match different specific instance situations. Hence, in this section, we could consider some key issues, like trust management, privacy protection, user management and encryption management, to ensure high QoS of cloud workflow systems. Besides, in former sections, such as data replication, data storage and so on, the security issue has been also considered from the perspective of other aspects of QoS. So, in the security management of cloud workflow system, we focus on the following contents to assure the key security of the whole system. In this section, we focus on privacy protection in cloud.

Firstly, for QoS constraint setting some constraints should be set in this beginning, such as privacy protection boundary. They are percentages to be totally protected. Secondly, for QoS service selection, privacy protection operates the selection process to get a reasonable security level on the basis of QoS constraint setting. Thirdly, for QoS consistency monitoring, in dynamic changing processes of cloud workflow instances, privacy protection constraints can be changing and should be monitored in the entire period. Privacy protection has to adjust itself based on trust management, and keep on considering changing data with private information in terms of data distributions or data compositions. Lastly, for QoS violation handling, as a consequential step of QoS consistency monitoring, this step should focus on these areas which are changing in the whole period and may get out of constraints in this first step—privacy protection boundary. So, in this step, we should execute the security service and mechanism selection step again under security constraints to turn the whole SwinDeW-C instance back into the right line.

4.7.1 Privacy Protection in Cloud

The privacy protection module plays a key role in keeping data security in distributed systems [4]. In cloud environments [56], the feature of computing and storing data in cloud brings more challenge to privacy protection in cloud workflow systems. Every user in a cloud workflow system is hardly to know every detail about one instance for the feature of virtualisation in cloud environment. So, we focus on an approach of privacy protection—noise obfuscation.

Although there are many service providers could protect their users' privacy, it cannot be ignored that a large number of "immoral" service providers are or will be an inherent part of an open cloud workflow environment. So, such service providers may and could record service information from a user and then collectively induce the user's privacy information without permissions from the user. Facing this serious risk, users should take some measures to aid them to protect their own privacy without cooperation from these service providers. For cloud workflow systems, it is unavoidable to deal with this risk. Noise obfuscation strategy belongs to these measures which can aids users to protect privacy at the client side. It can inject "noise" service information into real users' service information so that service providers could not distinguish which requests are real ones if their occurrence probabilities are about same. We use an example to illustrate the noise obfuscation strategy: a user often travels to "Sydney", hence checks the weather report regularly from a weather service in cloud before departures. The frequent appearance of service requests about the weather report for "Sydney" can reveal the privacy that the user usually goes to "Sydney". But if one system aids the user to inject other requests like "Perth" or "Darwin" into the "Sydney" queue, the service provider cannot realise which ones are real and which ones are "noise". It just sees a same style of service requests which should be responded and could not reveal the location privacy of the user. So, the privacy can be protected by the noise obfuscation strategy. For cloud workflow systems, generally, noise obfuscation could keep privacy safe in the processes of the data transactions between "vague" members in cloud workflow instances.

4.7.2 Trust Based Privacy Protection

Trust can be brought into discuss privacy protection in the "vague" environment [33]. As depicted in Fig. 4.5, we can investigate noise injection architecture for entire cooperative service processes in cloud environments. And it specialises in various single-service processes with service roles in cloud based on a trust model. The trust model and privacy risk are basic supporting functions to fulfil the architecture. Based on this, we can present our trust-based noise injection strategy for privacy protection in cloud, and it protects users' privacy during the entire process of services' cooperation. In the strategy, we use "noise" service requests to protect users' privacy in a cooperative service process by not only clients, but also other service providers. And the trust model and noise injection model are bridges to connect clients and services as a whole for noise injection architecture. The noise injection architecture is utilised to aid to describe cooperative service processes. It provides a supporting environment for our trust-based noise injection strategy. So, our strategy focuses on the procedure of cooperative service processes and protects users' privacy during entire cooperative service processes, especially for cloud workflow systems.

In [33], the noise injection architecture could be utilized to support the strategy in cloud computing environments.

In the viewpoint of control domain, we have three control domains in the whole architecture: individual control domain, semi-control domain and public domain which correspond to customer environment, control services environment and public services environment, separately. In cloud, these control domains report that who own and maintain these computing environments together. The individual control domain and semi-control domain are under the control of customers and some cloud managers, and our noise injection strategy for privacy protection has deployed in these two domains to be effective. In public domain, there are total unknown and uncontrolled in view of customers. It maybe locates in public cloud or other clouds.

In the viewpoint of virtualisation layer, we have three layers in the whole architecture: role layer, service layer and deploying layer which correspond to

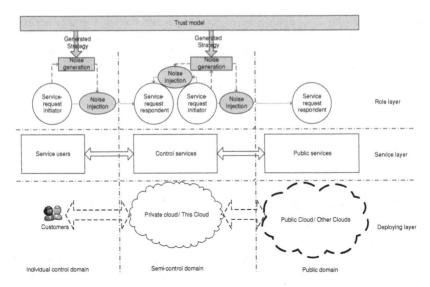

Fig. 4.5 Noise injection architecture in the cloud [33]

running environment, service environment and the environment to generate noise, separately.

What we focus on is the role layer. In this layer, on the ground of these roles of service-request initiator and service-request respondent, noise injections have highlighted to inject interactions between these roles. To generate these noises to protect privacy, these noise generation strategies which have been highlighted too are the innovative point of this book. And the detailed strategy is presented in Appendix D.

Chapter 5
Case Study: SwinDeW-C Cloud Workflow System

The previous chapters have given a general overview of cloud workflow system architecture, functionality and quality of service. In this chapter, we will demonstrate our SwinDeW-C cloud workflow system as a concrete case study to illustrate the design and development of a cloud workflow system for running large scale workflow applications. The literature review of some related research studies are discussed in Appendix E. The remainder of the chapter is organised as follows. Section 5.1 introduces our SwinDeW-G grid computing environment. Section 5.2 proposes the architecture for SwinDeW-C as well as SwinDeW-C peers. Section 5.3 presents the new components in SwinDeW-C for managing large scale workflow applications. Section 5.4 presents SwinDeW-C system prototype. Finally, Sect. 5.5 demonstrates some experimental results.

5.1 Overview of SwinDeW-G Environment

Before we present SwinDeW-C, some background knowledge about SwinDeW-G needs to be introduced. **Swin**burne **De**centralised **W**orkflow for **G**rid (SwinDeW-G) is a peer-to-peer based scientific grid workflow system running on the SwinGrid (Swinburne service Grid) platform [85].

An overall picture of SwinGrid is depicted in Fig. 5.1 (bottom plane). SwinGrid contains many grid nodes distributed in different places. Each grid node contains many computers including high performance PCs and/or supercomputers composed of significant numbers of computing units. The primary hosting nodes include the Swinburne CS3 (Centre for Complex Software Systems and Services) Node (which is now SUCCESS, Swinburne University Centre for Computing Engineering and Software Systems), the Swinburne ESR (Enterprise Systems Research laboratory) Node, the Swinburne Astrophysics Supercomputer Node, and the Beihang CROWN (China R&D environment Over Wide-area Network) Node in China. They are running either Linux, GT4 (Globus Toolkit) or CROWN grid

X. Liu et al., *The Design of Cloud Workflow Systems*,
SpringerBriefs in Computer Science, DOI: 10.1007/978-1-4614-1933-4_5,
© The Author(s) 2012

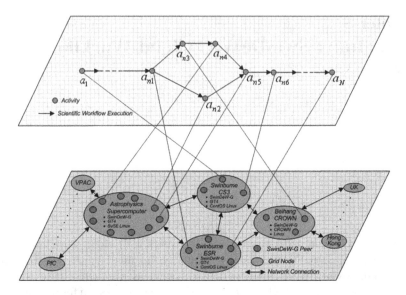

Fig. 5.1 SwinDeW-G environment

toolkit 2.5 where CROWN is an extension of GT4 with more middleware, and thus
is compatible with GT4. The CROWN Node is also connected to some other nodes
such as those at the Hong Kong University of Science and Technology, and at the
University of Leeds in the UK. The Swinburne Astrophysics Supercomputer Node
is cooperating with the Australian Platforms for Collaboration (PfC) and Victorian
Partnership for Advanced Computing (VPAC). Currently, SwinDeW-G is
deployed at primary hosting nodes as exemplified by the top plane of Fig. 5.1.
In SwinDeW-G, a scientific workflow is executed by different peers that may be
distributed at different grid nodes. As shown in Fig. 5.1, each grid node can have a
number of peers, and each peer can be simply viewed as a grid service. In the top
plane of Fig. 5.1, we show a sample of how a scientific workflow can be executed
in the grid computing environment.

The basic service unit in SwinDeW-G is a SwinDeW-G peer which runs as a
grid service along with other grid services. However, it communicates with other
peers via JXTA (http://www.sun.com/software/jxta/), a platform for p2p communication. As Fig. 5.2 shows, a SwinDeW-G peer consists of the following
components:

The Task Component manages the workflow tasks. It has two main functions.
First, it provides necessary information to the Flow Component for scheduling and
stores received tasks to Task Repository. Second, it determines the appropriate
time to start, execute and terminate a particular task. The resources that a workflow
task instance may require are stored in the Resource Repository.

The Flow Component interacts with all other modules. First, it receives the
workflows definition and then creates the instance definition. Second, it receives
tasks from other peers or redistributes them. Third, it decides whether to pass a

Fig. 5.2 Architecture of
SwinDeW-G peer

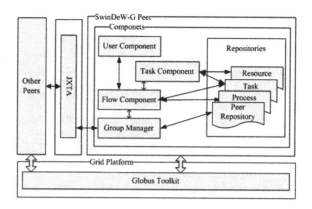

task to the Task Component to execute locally or distribute it to other peers. The
decision is made according to the capabilities and load of itself and other neighbours. And finally, it makes sure that all executions conform to the data dependency and control dependency of the process definitions which are stored in the
Process Repository and the Task Repository.

The Group Manager is the interface between the peer and JXTA. In JXTA, all
communications are conducted in terms of peer group, and the Group Manager
maintains the peer groups the peer has joined. The information of the peer groups
and the peers in them is stored in the Peer Repository. While a SwinDeW-G peer is
implemented as a grid service, all direct communications between peers are
conducted via p2p. Peers communicate to distribute information of their current
state and messages for process control such as heartbeat, process distribution,
process enactment etc.

The User component is the interface between the corresponding workflow users
and the workflow environment. In SwinDeW-G, its primary function is to allow
users to interfere with the workflow instances when exceptions occur.

Globus Toolkit serves as the grid service container of SwinDeW-G. Not only a
SwinDeW-G peer itself is a grid service located inside Globus Toolkit, the capabilities which are needed to execute certain tasks are also in the forms of grid services
that the system can access. That means when a task is assigned to a peer, Globus
Toolkit will be used to provide the required capability as grid service for that task.

5.2 SwinDeW-C System Architecture

In this section, the system architecture of SwinDeW-C is introduced. **Swin**burne
Decentralised **W**orkflow for **C**loud (SwinDeW-C) is built on SwinCloud cloud
computing infrastructure. SwinDeW-C inherits many features of its ancestor
SwinDeW-G but with significant modifications to accommodate the novel cloud
computing paradigm for managing large scale workflow applications.

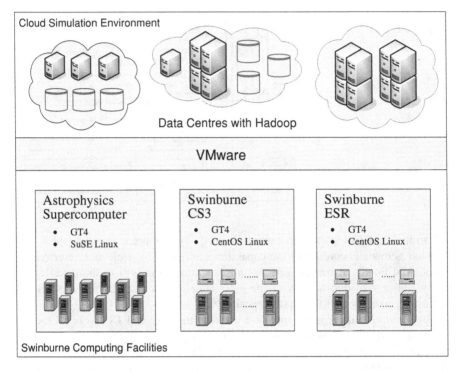

Fig. 5.3 SwinCloud infrastructure

5.2.1 SwinCloud Infrastructure

SwinCloud is a cloud computing simulation environment, on which SwinDeW-C is currently running. It is built on the computing facilities in Swinburne University of Technology and takes advantage of the existing SwinGrid systems. We install VMWare (http://www.vmware.com/) on SwinGrid, so that it can offer unified computing and storage resources. Utilising the unified resources, we set up data centres that can host applications. In the data centres, Hadoop (http://hadoop.apache.org/) is installed that can facilitate Map-Reduce computing paradigm and distributed data management. The architecture of SwinCloud is depicted in Fig. 5.3.

5.2.2 Architecture of SwinDeW-C

The architecture of SwinDeW-C is depicted in Fig. 5.4. As discussed earlier in Chap. 2, the general cloud architecture includes four basic layers from top to bottom: application layer (user applications), platform layer (middleware cloud

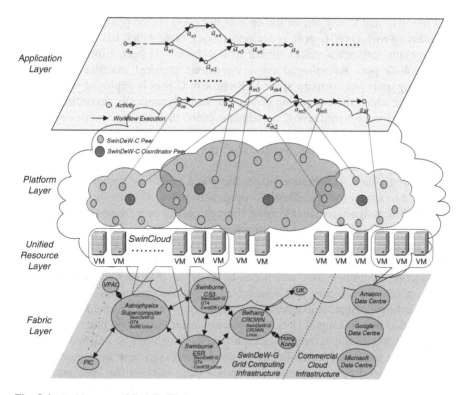

Application Layer

Platform Layer

Unified Resource Layer

Fabric Layer

Fig. 5.4 Architecture of SwinDeW-C

services to facilitate the development/deployment of user applications), unified resource layer (abstracted/encapsulated resources by virtualisation) and fabric layer (physical hardware resources). Accordingly, the architecture of SwinDeW-C can also be mapped to the four basic layers. Here, we present the lifecycle of an abstract workflow application to illustrate the system architecture. Note that here we focus on the system architecture, the introduction on the cloud management services (e.g. brokering, pricing, accounting, and virtual machine management) and other functional components are omitted here and will be introduced in the subsequent sections.

Users can easily get access to SwinDeW-C Web portal (as demonstrated in Sect. 5.4) via any electronic devices such as PC, laptop, PDA and mobile phone as long as they are connected to the Internet. Compared with SwinDeW-G which can only be accessed through a SwinDeW-G peer with pre-installed programs, the SwinDeW-C Web portal has greatly improved its usability. At workflow build-time stage, given the cloud workflow modelling tool provided by the Web portal on the application layer, workflow applications are modelled by users as cloud workflow specifications (consist of such as task definitions, process structures and QoS constraints). After workflow specifications are created (static verification tools for such as structure errors and QoS constraints may also be provided), they will be submitted to any one of the coordinator peers on the platform layer. Here, an ordinary SwinDeW-C peer is a cloud service node which has been equipped with specific software services similar to a SwinDeW-G peer. However, while a SwinDeW-G peer is deployed on a standalone physical machine with fixed computing units and memory space, a SwinDeW-C peer is deployed on a virtual machine of which the computing power can scale dynamically according to task request. As for the SwinDeW-C coordinator peers, they are super nodes equipped with additional workflow management services compared with ordinary Swin-DeW-C peers. Details about SwinDeW-C peers will be introduced in the next section.

At the run-time instantiation stage, the cloud workflow specification can be submitted to any of the SwinDeW-C coordinator peers. Afterwards, the workflow tasks will be assigned to suitable peers through peer to peer based communication between SwinDeW-C peers. Since the peer management such as peer join, peer leave and peer search, as well as the p2p based workflow execution mechanism, is the same as in the SwinDeW-G system environment. Therefore, the detailed introduction is omitted here which can be found in [85]. Before workflow execution, a coordinator peer will conduct an evaluation process on the submitted cloud workflow instances to determine whether they can be accepted or not given the specified non-functional QoS requirements under the current pricing model. It is generally assumed that functional requirements can always be satisfied given the theoretically unlimited scalability of cloud. In the case where users need to run their own special programs, they can upload them through the Web portal and these programs will be automatically deployed in the data centre by the resource manager. Here, a negotiation process between the user and the cloud workflow system may be conducted if the user submitted workflow instance is not acceptable to the workflow system due to the unacceptable offer on budgets or deadlines. The final negotiation result will be either the compromised QoS requirements or a failed submission of the cloud workflow instance. If all the task instances have been successfully allocated (i.e. acceptance messages are sent back to the coordinator peer from all the allocated peers), a cloud workflow instance may be completed with satisfaction of both functional and non-functional QoS requirements (if without exceptions). Hence, a cloud workflow instance is successfully instantiated.

Finally, at run-time execution stage, each task is executed by a SwinDeW-C peer. In cloud computing, the underlying heterogeneous resources are virtualised as unified resources (virtual machines). Each peer utilises the computing power provided by its virtual machine which can easily scale according to the request of workflow tasks. As can be seen in the unified resource layer of Fig. 5.4, the SwinCloud is built on the previous SwinGrid infrastructure at the fabric layer. Meanwhile, some of the virtual machines can be created with external commercial Infrastructure as Service (IaaS) cloud service providers such as Amazon, Google and Microsoft. During cloud workflow execution, workflow management tasks such as performance management, data management and security management are executed by the coordinator peers in order to achieve satisfactory system

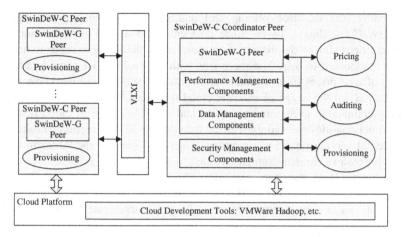

Fig. 5.5   Architecture of SwinDeW-C peers

performance. Users can get access to the final results as well as the running information of their submitted workflow instances at any time through the SwinDeW-C Web portal.

5.2.3 Functionalities of SwinDeW-C Peers

In this section we introduce the architecture of a SwinDeW-C peer. As we described above, SwinDeW-C is developed based on SwinDeW-G, where a SwinDeW-C peer has inherited most of the SwinDeW-G peer's components, including the components of task management, flow management, repositories, and the group management. Hence a SwinDeW-G peer plays as the core of a SwinDeW-C peer, which provides the basic workflow management components and communication components between peers. However, some improvements are also made for SwinDeW-C peers to accommodate the cloud computing environment. The architecture of the SwinDeW-C peers is depicted in Fig. 5.5.

Firstly, different from a SwinDeW-G peer, a SwinDeW-C peer runs on the cloud platform. The cloud platform is composed of unified resources, which means the computation and storage capabilities that a SwinDeW-C peer can dynamically scale up or down based on the applications' requirements. Unified resources are offered by cloud service providers and managed in resource pools, hence every SwinDeW-C peer has a provisioning component to dynamically apply and release the cloud resources. Meanwhile, through the SwinDeW-C coordinate peer, it can also scale out or in if necessary, i.e. to request the distribution of workflow activities to more or fewer SwinDeW-C peers in the same group. This is mainly realised through the APIs of VMWare management tools.

Secondly, the resource pricing and auditing components are equipped in SwinDeW-C coordinator peers. Since different cloud service providers may offer different prices, during the instantiation stage, a coordinator peer needs to have the pricing component to negotiate the prices with external service providers and set its own offered prices to its clients. Meanwhile, since the cloud workflow system needs to pay for the usage of external cloud resources, at the execution stage, an auditing component is required to record and audit the usage of cloud resources. These functionalities are mainly realised through the APIs of resource brokers and the external service provider's monitoring services such as the Amazon Cloud-Watch (http://aws.amazon.com/cloudwatch/).

Last but not least, the coordinator peer of SwinDeW-C also has new functional components related to cloud workflow management. As introduced in Sect. 2.2, the system has new requirements for handling the large scale workflow applications. To meet these new requirements, components of performance management, data management and security management are added to the SwinDeW-C coordinator peer. More detailed descriptions of these components will be given in the following section.

5.3 QoS Management Components in SwinDeW-C

In this section, we introduce the QoS management components in SwinDeW-C. Specifically, the three QoS management components including performance management, data management (data storage and data replication) and security management are introduced. Note that in SwinDeW-C, since the cost management on data storage and reliability management on data replication are both working on the cloud datasets, they are integrated into the data management component.

5.3.1 Performance Management in SwinDeW-C

As introduced in Sect. 4.4, the performance management in SwinDeW-C includes four basic tasks: the setting of temporal constraints, the selection of candidate cloud services, the monitoring of workflow execution against QoS constraint violations, and the handling of QoS constraint violations.

Temporal Constraint Setting: In SwinDeW-C QoS management component, a probabilistic strategy is designed for setting temporal QoS constraints at workflow build time [49]. Specifically, with a probability based temporal consistency model, the one global or several coarse-grained temporal constraints are assigned based on the negotiation result between clients and service providers. Afterwards, fine-grained temporal constraints for individual workflow activities can be derived automatically based on these coarse-grained ones.

Candidate Service Selection: Given the fine-grained constraints for response time assigned in the first step, a set of candidate services which satisfy the constraints can be searched by the cloud resource broker from the cloud [17]. Meanwhile, since different service providers may offer different prices, and there are often other QoS constraints such as reliability and security to be considered at the same time, a ranking strategy is designed to determine the best candidate for runtime execution. Furthermore, considering to the dynamic nature of cloud computing as well as the performance and reliability requirements for managing large numbers of business processes, a set of backup/redundant services should also be reserved during service selection. In fact, many cloud service providers such as Amazon provides special discount price for reserved resources.[1]

Checkpoint Selection and Temporal Verification: At workflow run time, a checkpoint selection strategy and a temporal verification strategy are provided to monitor the workflow execution against the violation of temporal constraints. Temporal verification is to check the temporal correctness of workflow execution states (detecting temporal violations) given a temporal consistency model. Meanwhile, in order to save the overall QoS management cost, temporal verification should be conducted only on selected activity points. In SwinDeW-C, a minimum time redundancy based checkpoint selection strategy [22, 23] is employed which can select only necessary and sufficient checkpoints (those where temporal violations take place).

Violation Handling: After a temporal violation is detected, violation handling strategies are required to recover the error states. Unlike functional errors which are normally prevented by duplicated instances or handled by rollback and re-execution, non-functional QoS errors such as temporal violations can only be recovered by compensation, i.e. to reduce or ideally remove the current time delays by decreasing the durations of the subsequent workflow activities. Since the previous activities have already been finished, there is no way in the real world that any action can reduce their running time. In SwinDeW-C, for minor temporal violations, the time deficit allocation (TDA) strategy [21] is employed which can remove the current time deficits by borrowing the time redundancy of the subsequent activities. As for major temporal violations, the ant colony optimisation based two stage workflow local rescheduling (ACOWR) strategy [48] is employed which can decrease the duration of the subsequent workflow segments through ant colony optimisation based workflow rescheduling.

In SwinDeW-C, by constant monitoring of the workflow instance and effective handling of temporal violations along workflow execution, satisfactory temporal QoS can be delivered with low violation rates of both global and local temporal constraints. Similar to temporal QoS management, the management tasks for other QoS constraints are being investigated. Meanwhile, since some of them such as cost and security are partially addressed in the data management and security management components, some functions will be shared among these components.

---

[1] http://aws.amazon.com/ec2/reserved-instances/

5.3.2 Data Management (Storage and Replication) in SwinDeW-C

Data management component in SwinDeW-C consists of three basic tasks: data storage, data placement and data replication.

Data Storage: In this component, a dependency based cost-effective data storage strategy is facilitated to store the application data [88]. The strategy utilises the data provenance information of the workflow instances. Data provenance in workflows is a kind of important metadata, in which the dependencies between datasets are recorded [72]. The dependency depicts the derivation relationship between the application datasets. In cloud workflow systems, after the execution of tasks, some intermediate datasets may be deleted to save the storage cost, but sometimes they have to be regenerated for either reuse or reanalysis [15]. Data provenance records the information of how the datasets have been generated. Furthermore, regeneration of the intermediate datasets from the input data may be very time consuming, and therefore carry a high computation cost. With data provenance information, the regeneration of the demanding dataset may start from some stored intermediated datasets instead. In a cloud workflow system, data provenance is recorded during workflow execution. Taking advantage of data provenance, we can build an Data Dependency Graph (IDG) based on data provenance [88]. All the intermediate datasets once generated in the system, whether stored or deleted, their references are recorded in the DDG. Based on the DDG, we can calculate the generation cost of every dataset in the cloud workflows. By comparing the generation cost and storage cost, the storage strategy can automatically decide whether a dataset should be stored or deleted in the cloud system to reduce the system cost, no matter this dataset is a new dataset, regenerated dataset or stored dataset in the system.

Data Placement: In this component, a data placement strategy is facilitated to place the application data that can reduce the data movement during the workflows' execution. In cloud computing systems, the infrastructure is hidden from users. Hence, for application data, the system will decide where to store them. In the strategy, we initially adapt the k-means clustering algorithm for data placement in cloud workflow systems based on data dependency. Cloud workflows can be complex, one task might require many datasets for execution; furthermore, one dataset might also be required by many tasks. If some datasets are always used together by many tasks, we say that these datasets are dependant on each other. In our strategy, we try to keep these datasets in one data centre, so that when tasks were scheduled to this data centre, most, if not all, of the data needed are stored locally. Our data placement strategy has two algorithms, one for the build-time stage and one for the runtime stage of scientific workflows. In the build-time stage algorithm, we construct a dependency matrix for all the application data, which represents the dependencies between all the datasets. Then we use the BEA algorithm [57] to cluster the matrix and partition it that datasets in every partition are highly dependent upon each other. We distribute the partitions into k data centres, which are initially as the partitions of the k-means algorithm at run time stage. At runtime, our clustering algorithm deals with the newly generated data that will be needed by other tasks. For every newly generated dataset, we calculate its dependencies with all k data centres, and move the data to the data centre that has the highest dependency with it.

Data Replication: In this component, a dynamic data replication strategy is facilitated to guarantee data reliability and the fast data access of the cloud workflow systems. Keeping some replicas of the application data is essential for data reliability in cloud storage. Static replication can guarantee the data reliability by keeping a fixed number of replicas of the application data, but in a cloud environment, different application data have different usage frequency, where the strategy has to be dynamic to replicate the application data based on their usage rates. In large scale workflow applications, many parallel tasks will simultaneously access the same dataset on one data centre. The possible limitation of network bandwidth in one data centre would be a bottleneck for the whole cloud workflow system. If we have several replicas in different data centres, this bottleneck will be eliminated. Hence the data replication will always keep a fix number of copies of all the datasets across different data centres to guarantee reliability and dynamically add new replicas for each dataset to guarantee data availability. Furthermore, the placement of the replicas is based on data dependency, which is the same as the data placement component, and how many replicas a dataset should have is based on the usage rate of this dataset.

5.3.3 Security Management in SwinDeW-C

To address the security issues for the safe running of SwinDeW-C, the security management component is designed. As a type of typical distributed computing system, trust management for SwinDeW-C peers is very important and plays the most important role in security management. Besides, there are some other security issues that we should consider from such as user and data perspectives. Specifically, there are three modules in the security management component: trust management, user management, privacy protection and encryption management system.

Trust Management: The goal of the trust management module is to manage the relations between one SwinDeW-C peer and its neighbouring peers. For example, to process a workflow instance, a SwinDeW-C peer must cooperate with its neighbouring peers to run this instance. Due to the high QoS requirements of large scale workflow applications, peer management in SwinDeW-C should be supported by the trust management during workflow runtime. The trust management module acts like a consultant. This module can evaluate some tasks and give some advices about the cooperated relation between one peer and other peers for each instance of a specific task. Firstly, peer evaluation makes trust assessment of other neighbouring peers. Secondly, task evaluation makes assessment of re-assignment of the task to other peers. Then the two evaluation scores are combined by the trust evaluation to reach the conclusion whether this neighbouring peer has adequate trust to take this task. Besides, we design a rule base. For instance, a specific task must not be assigned to one specific neighbouring peer, and this is a simple rule. The rule base is a complement to the previous value-based trust evaluation to fit the real situation.

Privacy Protection: The privacy protection module is to keep customer private information safe in the process of one SwinDeW-C instance. We can utilise trust management module as a basis of this module to control the noise obfuscation process [33]. So, this module can be applied in every SwinDeW-C peer, generates and injects noise data in transactions of SwinDeW-C instances to conceal real customer private information. For example, a high trust level means a low level of noise utilisation, and vice versa.

User Management: The user management module is an essential piece in every system. In cloud workflow systems, to support the function of access control [6], a user base is a database which stores all user identity and log information to control submitted service requests. In addition, an authority manager controls the permissions for users to submit some special service requests. To the designer of a cloud workflow system, the user management may not only a user base to access control for the whole system, but also a bunch of methods to realise the function of pricing mechanism. Because the pay-as-you-go style of cloud is the key issue to express the advantage of cloud. Besides, for the perspective of security, the usage of users should be records and be analysed to find some abnormal behaviours about users. It may be a malicious user, or an account disclosure. It is necessary to be considered to operate it or just reserve upgrade interfaces by a designer of a cloud workflow system to keep its security.

Encryption Management System: Given cloud workflow systems members may be located within different geographical local networks, it is important to ensure the data security in the process of data transfer by encryption. In our cloud workflow systems—SwinDeW-C, we choose the PGP tool GnuPG (http://www.gnupg.org/) to ensure secure commutation. In common applications, current encryption components or algorithms can match the data security requirement. But the execution of encryption function should consume a lot of resources on computing and storage, especially in data intensive instances. So, it is a trade-off between data security and resource cost. For the designer of a cloud workflow system, it is necessary to design a mechanism to make the balance flexible with the actual computing situations. Sometimes users could take part in this process. In other words, users could decide and control the operation of encryption in the run-time of a cloud workflow instance. For example, for one specific step of this instance, users would decide whether to use encryption to protect data or not, on the basis of trust management.

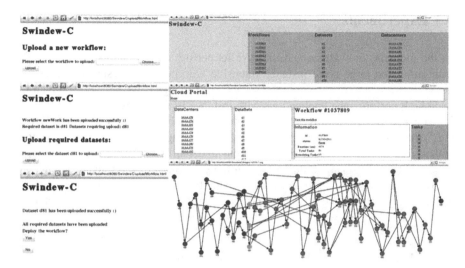

Fig. 5.6 SwinDeW-C web portal

5.4 SwinDeW-C System Prototype

Based on the design discussed above, we have built a primitive prototype of SwinDeW-C. The prototype is developed in Java and currently running on the SwinCloud simulation environment. In the SwinDeW-C prototype, we have inherited most of SwinDeW-G functions, and further implemented the new components of SwinDeW-C, so that it can adapt to the cloud computing environment. Furthermore, we have built a Web portal for SwinDeW-C, by which users and system administrators can access the cloud resources and manage the applications of SwinDeW-C. As shown in Fig. 5.6, the Web portal provides many interfaces to support both system users and administrators with the following tasks, specifically for the system users:

1) browse the existing datasets that reside in different cloud service providers' data centres;
2) upload their application data to and download the result data from the cloud storage;
3) create and deploy workflows to SwinDeW-C system using the modelling tools;
4) monitor the workflows' execution.

For system administrators:

1) coordinate the workflows' execution by triggering the scheduling strategies;
2) manage the application datasets by triggering the data placement strategies;
3) handle the execution exceptions and QoS violations by triggering the workflow exception handling and QoS violation handling strategies.

5.5 Experiments

At the moment, to evaluate and improve its performance, a number of test cases with simulated large scale instance intensive workflows are designed and being tested in SwinDeW-C, including the securities exchange workflow and some large scale high performance applications with instance intensive sub-processes such as a weather forecast workflow [15] and a pulsar searching workflow in Astrophysics [52]. Specifically, the effectiveness of the QoS management components is tested with various sizes of cloud workflows and under different environment settings. Here, we only demonstrate the results on the evaluation of time management (on performance) and cost management (on data storage) as two representative QoS management components to verify the effectiveness of the SwinDeW-C system.

5.5.1 Evaluation on Performance Management

In order to evaluate the performance of SwinDeW-C, we have simulated a large number of workflow instances running in parallel. Each workflow instance can have 20–50 activities, and the total number of cloud workflow activities ranges from 500 to 20,000. The structures of the workflow instance are randomly generated according to the sub-processes of the securities exchange workflow. The activity durations are generated based on the statistics and deliberately extended by a mixture of representative distribution models such as normal, uniform and exponential to reflect the performance of different virtual machines. The number of virtual machines is increased with the number of workflow activities where the length of the job list for each virtual machine is bounded with a random number from 10 to 20. The process structures are specified according to the workflow segments similar to the securities exchange business process introduced in Sect. 1.4. For each workflow instance, an overall temporal constraint is assigned. The strategy for setting temporal constraint is adopted from the work in [49] where a normal percentile is used to specify temporal constraints and denotes the expected probability for on-time completion. Here, we conduct three rounds of independent experiments where the temporal constraints are set with different normal percentiles of 1.00, 1.15 and 1.28 which denotes the probability of 84.1, 87.5 and 90.0% for on-time completion without any handling strategies on temporal violations (denoted as COM (1.00), COM (1.15) and COM (1.28)). For the comparison purpose, we record global violation rates under natural situations, i.e. without any handling strategies (denoted as NIL), and compared with that of TDA strategy [21] and our three-level handling strategy as introduced in Sect. 4.3 (denoted as Framework where the three violation handling strategies are implemented automatically according to the levels of temporal violations [13]). In TDA + ACOWR, the maximum iteration times for ACOWR are set as 2. Each round of experiment is executed for 100 times to get the average violation rates.

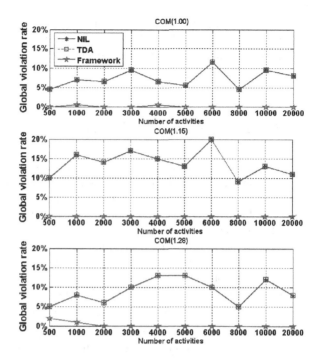

Fig. 5.7 Global temporal violation rate

The initial experimental results on system performance have shown that close to 0% violation rates of global and local temporal constraints can be achieved in SwinDeW-C, thanks to its structured p2p based decentralised management, effective provision of computing resources and advanced QoS management [51, 53]. Here, we only demonstrate part of the experimental results on the global violation rate (the violation of the final deadline) which is an overall measurement for workflow execution. Figure 5.7 shows the results on global violation rates. Since TDA can only delay the temporal violations without actual compensating the time deficits, it may handle local violations but has no effect on global violations. Therefore, the global violation rates for NIL and TDA are overlapping. The global violation rates for NIL and TDA behave very unstably but increase roughly with the number of activities while decreasing with the value of normal percentiles. The average global violation rates for NIL and TDA in each round are 14.6, 13.8 and 9.0% respectively. With our performance framework, the global violation rate is kept close to zero since most local temporal violations are handled automatically along workflow executions. The average global violation rates of our performance framework in each round are 0.2, 0.0 and 0.3% respectively, i.e. an overall average of 0.167%. Accordingly, the reductions in the global violation rates are 14.4, 13.8 and 8.7% respectively, with an average of 12.3%, which is very significant. Therefore, with the implementation of our concrete performance framework, the global violation rates of workflow instances can be significantly reduced, which effectively verifies its satisfactory effectiveness in the support of temporal QoS in cloud workflow systems.

To conclude, given the above results which show that most of the workflow instances are completed in time, we can claim that our SwinDeW-C cloud workflow system can effectively manage the execution of instance intensive business processes.

5.5.2 Evaluation on Data Storage Management

The datasets storage strategy addressed here is generic. It can be used in any scientific applications with different price models of cloud services. In this section, we demonstrate the simulation results that we conduct on the SwinCloud environment. First, we use general (random) DDG and datasets to demonstrate the cost-effectiveness comparison of our strategies. Then we utilise our strategies to the specific pulsar searching application described in Sect. 1.4, and use the real world data to demonstrate how our strategies work in storing the application datasets of the pulsar searching workflow.

In addition to store none and all datasets strategies, we compare the cost-effectiveness of different storage strategies as follows:

1) Usage based strategy, in which we store the datasets that are most often used.
2) Generation cost based strategy, in which we store the datasets that incur the highest generation cost.
3) Cost rate based strategy reported in [88], in which we store the datasets by comparing their own generation cost rate and storage cost rate.
4) Local-optimisation based strategy reported in [89, 91], in which we also utilise the CTT-SP algorithm and achieve a localised optimum for storing a large DDG.

5.5.2.1 General Random Simulations and Results

The random simulations are conducted on randomly generated DDG with datasets of random sizes, generation times and usage frequencies. Due to the page limit, we only present some representative results in this section without losing generality. We use the DDG with 50 datasets, each with a random size from 100 GB to 1 TB. The generation time is also random, from 1 h to 10 h. The usage frequency is again randomly from 1 day to 10 days (time between every usage). The prices of cloud services follow the well-known Amazon's cost model, i.e. $0.1 per CPU instance hour for computation and $0.15 per gigabyte per month for storage. To reflect users' delay tolerance, we set a random time tolerance (T_i) from 10 h to one day and a random cost parameter of delay tolerance (λ_i) from 0.7 to 1 to every datasets in the DDG. All these random parameters are generated with the uniform distribution. For other distributions, we have similar results in our experiment.

Fig. 5.8 Cost-effectiveness comparison of different storage strategies

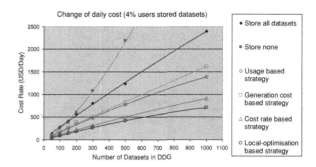

To reflect the users' preferences, we randomly select 4% of the datasets to store in the system based on users' preferences.

With the settings above, we ran simulations under different numbers of datasets in the DDG. Figure 5.8 shows the increases of the daily cost rates of different strategies as the number of datasets grows in the DDG. From Fig. 5.8, we can see that the "store none" and "store all" strategies are very cost ineffective, since their daily cost rates grow fast as the datasets number grows. The cost rate based strategy has a better performance than both the generation cost based strategy and usage based strategy. The local-optimisation based strategy is the most cost-effective datasets storage strategy, and it reduces the total cost rate by over 20% on average comparing to the cost rate based strategy.

5.5.2.2 Specific Pulsar Searching Simulation and Results

The random simulations demonstrate the general performance of our datasets storage strategies. Next, we utilise it to the pulsar searching workflow introduced in Sect. 1.4 and show how it works in this real world scientific application.

In the pulsar example, for one execution of the workflow, six datasets are generated. Scientists may need to re-analyse these datasets, or reuse them in new workflows and generate new datasets. The DDG of this pulsar searching workflow is shown in Fig. 5.9, as well as the sizes and generation times of these datasets. The generation times of the datasets are from running this workflow on Swinburne Astrophysics Supercomputer, and for simulation, we assume that in the cloud, the generation times of these datasets are the same. Furthermore, we again assume that the cost of cloud services follow Amazon clouds' price.

From Swinburne Astrophysics research group, we understand that the "De-dispersion files" is the most useful dataset. Based on these files, many accelerating and seeking methods can be used to search pulsar candidates. Based on the scenario, we set the "De-dispersion files" to be used once every 4 days and other datasets to be used once every 10 days. Furthermore, we assume new datasets are generated on the 10th and 20th days, indicated as sub DDG_1 and DDG_2 in Fig. 5.9. Based on this setting, we run the above mentioned simulation strategies and

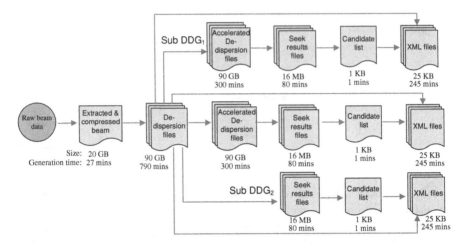

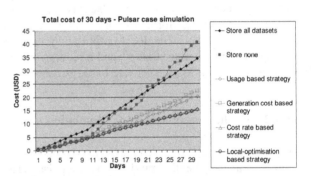

Fig. 5.9 DDG of pulsar searching workflow

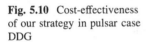

Fig. 5.10 Cost-effectiveness of our strategy in pulsar case DDG

calculate the total costs of the system for one branch of the pulsar searching workflow of processing one piece of observation data in 30 days as shown in Fig. 5.10.

Figure 5.10 shows a consistent result with the previous general random simulations, where the cost rate based strategy also has a good performance in this pulsar searching application and the most cost-effective datasets storage strategy is still our local-optimisation based strategy.

Appendix A
Performance Management Strategies

A.1 Probability Range for Recoverable Temporal Violations

The detailed definition for the probability based temporal consistency state is presented in [53] and hence omitted in this chapter. Here, we focus on the introduction of the probability range for statistically recoverable temporal violations. As depicted in Fig. A.1, the effective range for light-weight temporal violation handling is defined as (0.13, 99.87%) which is represented by the shadowed area. The reason can be explained as follows. Since the maximum and minimum duration for each activity are defined as $D(a_i) = \mu_i + 3\sigma_i$ and $d(a_i) = \mu_i - 3\sigma_i$ respectively, as explained in our hybrid estimation method and proved in [50], the overall workflow execution time can be estimated with the normal distribution model and has a statistical lower bound of $\mu - 3\sigma$ (with 0.13% consistency) and an upper bound of $\mu + 3\sigma$ (with 99.87% consistency) where μ and σ are the joint normal mean and standard deviation respectively for the durations of all activities included. In practice, at scientific workflow runtime, temporal violation handling is only triggered in the probability consistency range of (0.13, θ%) as shown in the area marked with upwards diagonal lines in Fig. A.1, while the probability consistency range of (θ, 99.87%) marked with downwards diagonal lines requires no action. Here, the threshold of θ% denotes the minimum acceptable temporal consistency and it is usually specified through the negotiation between users and service providers for setting local and global temporal constraints [49]. In practice, θ% is normally around or above 84.13%, i.e. $\mu + \sigma$. Therefore, if the current temporal consistency of α% (α% Consistency) is larger than θ%, including AC (Absolute Consistency), no action is required since the contract still holds. Otherwise, temporal violation handling is triggered to compensate the time deficit. In other words, a potential temporal violation is deemed as detected when the current temporal consistency state is below the threshold of θ%. However, when α% is below 0.13%, i.e. AI (Absolute

X. Liu et al., *The Design of Cloud Workflow Systems*,
SpringerBriefs in Computer Science, DOI: 10.1007/978-1-4614-1933-4,
© The Author(s) 2012

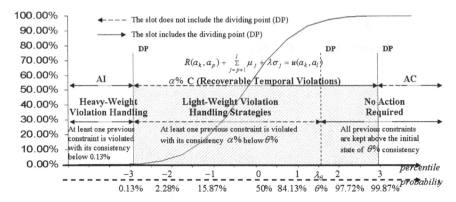

Fig. A.1 Statistically recoverable temporal violations

Inconsistency), instead of light-weight temporal violation handling, heavy-weight temporal violation handling strategies such as resource recruitment or workflow restructure must be implemented since the time remaining before temporal violation is smaller than the minimum completion time that the current scientific workflow system could statistically achieve without an expensive temporal violation handling process. Therefore, AI violations can be regarded as statistically non-recoverable temporal violations.

The probability consistency range where light-weight temporal violation handling is statistically effective is defined as (0.13, 99.87%). At scientific workflow runtime, based on temporal QoS contracts, light-weight temporal violation handling is only triggered when the probability of current temporal consistency state is within the range of (0.13, θ%) where θ% is the bottom-line temporal consistency state.

A.2 Minimum Probability Time Redundancy

After we have identified the effective probability consistency range for temporal violation handling, the next issue is to determine at which activity point to check for the temporal consistency so that a temporal violation can be detected in the first place. Here, a necessary and sufficient checkpoint selection strategy is proposed. First, the definitions of probability time redundancy and minimum probability time redundancy are presented.

Definition A.1 (*Probability Time Redundancy for Single Workflow Activity*).
At activity point a_p between a_i and $a_j (i \leq j)$, let $U(a_i, a_j)$ be of β%C with the percentile of λ_β which is above the threshold of θ% with the percentile of λ_θ. Then the probability time redundancy of $U(a_i, a_j)$ at a_p is defined as $PTR(U(a_i, a_j), a_p) = u(a_i, a_j) - [R(a_i, a_p) + \theta(a_{p+1}, a_j)]$. Here, $\theta(a_{p+1}, a_j) = \sum_{k=p+1}^{j} (\mu_k + \lambda_\theta \sigma_k)$.

Definition A.2 (*Minimum Probability Time Redundancy*)

Let U_1, U_2, ..., U_N be N upper bound constraints and all of them cover a_p. Then, at a_p, the minimum probability time redundancy is defined as the minimum of all probability time redundancies of U_1, U_2, ..., U_N and is represented as $MPTR(a_p) = Min\{PTR(U_s, a_p)|s = 1, 2, ..., N\}$.

The purpose of defining minimum probability time redundancy is to detect the earliest possible temporal violations. Based on Definition A.2, Theorem A.1 is presented to locate the exact temporal constraint which has the temporal consistency state below the $\theta\%$ bottom line.

Theorem A.1 *At activity point a_p, if $R(a_p) > \theta(a_p) + MPTR(a_{p-1})a$, then at least one of the temporal constraints is violated and it is exactly the one whose time redundancy at a_{p-1} is $MPTR(a_{p-1})$.*

Proof Suppose that $U(a_k, a_l)$ is an upper bound constraint whose probability is above the threshold before execution of a_p ($k < p < l$) and it is the one with $MPTR(a_{p-1})$. Then, according to Definition A.1, at a_{p-1}, we have $u(a_k, a_l) > R(a_k, a_{p-1}) + \theta(a_p, a_l)$ and $MPTR(a_{p-1}) = u(a_k, a_l) - R(a_k, a_{p-1}) - \theta(a_p, a_l)$. Now, assume that at activity a_p, we have $R(a_p) > \theta(a_p) + MPTR(a_{p-1})$ which means $R(a_p) > \theta(a_p) + u(a_k, a_l) - R(a_k, a_{p-1}) - \theta(a_p, a_l)$, and that is $u(a_k, a_l) < R(a_p) + R(a_k, a_{p-1}) + \theta(a_p, a_l) - \theta(a_p)$ where the right hand side equals $R(a_k, a_p) + \theta(a_{p-1}, a_l)$. Since $R(a_k, a_p) + \theta(a_{p-1}, a_l) < R(a_k, a_p) + \theta(a_{p+1}, a_l)$, we have $u(a_k, a_l) < R(a_k, a_p) + \theta(a_{p+1}, a_l)$ and this results in a probability of temporal consistency which is lower than that of $\theta\%$ where $u(a_k, a_l) = R(a_k, a_p) + \theta(a_{p+1}, a_l)$. Therefore, a potential temporal violation is detected and it is exactly the one whose time redundancy at a_{p-1} is $MPTR(a_{p-1})$. Thus, the theorem holds.

A.3 Temporal Checkpoint Selection and Temporal Verification Process

Based on Theorem A.1, we further present Theorem A.2 which describes our temporal checkpoint selection strategy followed by the proof of its necessity and sufficiency.

Theorem A.2 (Necessary and Sufficient Temporal Checkpoint Selection Strategy)

Within the consistency range of $(0.13 < \alpha < 99.87\%)$, at activity a_p, if $R(a_p) > \theta(a_p) + MPTR(a_{p-1})$, we select a_p as a temporal checkpoint, otherwise, we do not select a_p as a checkpoint. This strategy is of necessity, i.e. all checkpoints selected along workflow execution are necessary, and of sufficiency, i.e. there are no omitted checkpoints.

Proof According to Theorem A.1, once we select an activity, say a_p as a checkpoint, there must be at least one temporal constraint which has potential temporal violations detected at a_p and it is exactly the one whose time redundancy at a_{p-1} is $MPTR(a_{p-1})$. That is to say, selecting a_p as a checkpoint is necessary. Thus, the necessity property holds.

With an activity point a_p, we consider it as a checkpoint only if $R(a_p) > \theta(a_p) + MPTR(a_{p-1})$, i.e. $R(a_p) > \theta(a_p) + u(a_i, a_j) - [R(a_i, a_p) + \theta(a_{p+1}, a_j)]$. According to Definition A.2, if we assume that $u(a_i, a_j)$ is the constraint where minimum probability time redundancy occurs, then $R(a_p) > u(a_i, a_j) - [R(a_i, a_{p-1}) + \theta(a_p, a_j)]$. According to Definition A.1, Definition A.2 and the probability consistency range of $(0.13, \theta\%)$ where temporal violation handling needs to be triggered, we do not need to select a_p as a checkpoint if $R(a_i, a_p) \leq u(a_i, a_j) - \sum_{k=p}^{j} (\mu_k + \lambda_\theta \sigma_k)$ which means the probability consistency is above $\theta\%$, that is $R(a_p) \leq u(a_i, a_j) - [\theta(a_p, a_j) - R(a_i, a_{p-1})]$ which is $R(a_p) \leq \theta(a_p) + MPTR(a_{p-1})$. Therefore, no checkpoints are omitted. Thus, the sufficiency property holds.

Here, we also adopt the method of Dynamic Obtaining of Minimum Time Redundancy (DOMTR) [23]. Based on some initial values which are set up during the runtime instantiation stage, DOMTR can compute the minimum probability time redundancy on the fly along scientific workflow execution with minimal computation. Based on DOMTR, the computation of our checkpoint selection strategy is basically one or two subtractions or comparisons at each activity covered by one or more upper bound constraints. Therefore, as proved in [23], the computation cost is basically negligible.

To conclude, our checkpoint selection strategy strictly ensures that a checkpoint is selected only when current temporal consistency is below the minimum acceptable threshold. Meanwhile, since our temporal verification strategy is aware of the effective probability consistency range and can determine the fine-grained levels of temporal violations, it also ensures that statistically the time deficit can be compensated by light-weight temporal violation handling.

A.4 A Novel General Two-Stage Local Workflow Rescheduling Strategy for Recoverable Temporal Violations

Given the two fundamental requirements of automation and cost-effectiveness, the temporal violation handling strategies that we mainly investigate in this chapter are metaheuristics based workflow rescheduling algorithms. With metaheuristics based rescheduling algorithms, temporal violations are tackled by rescheduling the current Task-to-Resource assignment. Note that in cloud computing environments, computing resources are generally delivered as virtual machines (VMs). Therefore, in this chapter, Task-to-Resource assignment and Task-Resource list are interchangeable with Task-to-VM assignment or Task-VM list respectively. For workflow rescheduling, the following two challenges need to be considered: (1) the balance between the handling of temporal violations and the on-time completion of other workflow instances; (2) the suitable size of the Task-Resource list for cost-effective rescheduling. The reason why we do not consider heuristics based scheduling algorithms in this scenario is mainly as follows:

1. Heuristics based scheduling algorithms can only optimise one objective at a time. Meanwhile, it is based on local optimisation where it can choose the best candidates at each local step for the optimisation objective. However, the generated solution is not necessarily the best solution for the optimisation objective in an overall sense.
2. From the viewpoint of metaheuristics based scheduling algorithms, the process of heuristics based scheduling algorithms is to construct valid solutions. Since metaheuristics based scheduling algorithms can use the valid solutions generated by heuristic scheduling algorithms as the initial input solution, the optimisation capability of metaheuristics based scheduling algorithm is theoretically guaranteed to be better than heuristic scheduling algorithms.

To address the above two challenges, a novel general two-stage workflow local rescheduling strategy is designed for handing temporal violations. The pseudo-code for the general strategy is presented in Fig. A.2.

Here, "two-stage" means a two-stage searching process to strike a balance between the handling of temporal violations and the on-time completion of other workflow instances while "local" means the rescheduling of "local" workflow segments with existing resources. To handle temporal violations, the key optimisation objective is to maximise the compensation time, i.e. the difference of the scheduled execution time before and after rescheduling, in order to decrease the time deficit. After rescheduling, the activities for the violated workflow instance will be allocated with resources of higher performance and/or given earlier time slots in the job queue for execution. However, if we only focus on the violated workflow instance, the execution time of other workflow instances could be delayed and may violate temporal constraints of their own, if any. Therefore, a balance between the handling of temporal violations and the on-time completion of other workflow instances needs to be considered in scientific workflow systems. Otherwise, the overall temporal QoS of scientific workflow systems will be potentially deteriorated. As for local rescheduling, the first task is to identify the suitable size of the Task-Resource list. Our strategy only utilises existing local resources which are currently deployed in the system instead of recruiting additional resources outside the system. Meanwhile, unlike global rescheduling which modifies the global Task-Resource list for the entire workflow instance, we only focus on the local workflow segment and optimise the integrated Task-Resource list. Here, the local workflow segment is defined as the set of workflow activities between the next activity of a necessary and sufficient checkpoint (the activity point where a temporal violation occurs) [24] and the end activity of the next local temporal constraint. As depicted in Fig. A.3, the integrated Task-Resource list is an integrated collection of local resources and the integrated Directed Acyclic Graph (DAG) task graph which defines the precedence relationships of all the activities in the local workflow segment and their co-allocated activities. Here, co-allocated activities are those which have been allocated to the same resources.

Strategy: Two-Stage Local Workflow Rescheduling

Input: Time deficit detected at activity a_p $TD(a_p)$

Integrated Task-Resource list $L\{(a_i, R_j) \mid i = p+1,...p+n, j = 1,2,..K\}$;
DAG task graphs $DAG\{G_i \mid a_j \leq a_m\}$
Activity duration models $M\{\mu_i, \sigma_i^2\}$
Resource peers $R\{R_i, ES(R_i), Cost(R_i) \mid i = 1,2,...K\}$

Output: Rescheduled task-resource list

// **Stage 1: Optimising the makespan and cost for the integrated task-resource list through one metaheuristic algorithm**

1)   *INITILISATION*();

//Running of metaheuristic rescheduling algorithms to minimise both makespan and cost of the integrated task-resource list

2) While (stopping condition is not met)

    {

3)   *Run(Metaheuristic)*;

    }

// return the best-so-far solution and record into the *SolutionSet*

4)   *Return(Solution, SolutionSet)*;

    }

// **Stage 2: Searching for the *BestSolution* from *SolutionSet***

5) While (not end of the *SolutionSet*)

    {

// compare the compensation time of each *Solution* with the time deficit, discard the *Solution* if it is smaller than the time deficit

6)   *COMPARE(Solution.ct, TD(a_p))*;

// compare all remained *Solution* and set *BestSolution* as the one with the minimun cost

7)   *BestSolution = Min(Solution.cost)*;

    }

8) Return the *BestSolution*;

// return the rescheduled integrated task-resource list and deploy

9)   *Deploy(L)*;

Fig. A.2 Two-stage local workflow rescheduling strategy

For example, in Fig. A.3, local workflow segment contains activity a_{p+1} to a_{p+7} and they are allocated to four different resources R_1 to R_4. Each resource maintains a local Task-List by its own scheduler given its input job queue. When temporal violation handling is triggered, the workflow management system will acquire the current Task-List of R_1 to R_4 and can automatically combine them into an integrated DAG task graph which consists of all the tasks, for instance, a total of n tasks, by assigning a pseudo start activity a_{Start} and pseudo end activity a_{End}. Therefore, an integrated Task-Resource list $L\{(a_i, R_j) \mid i = p+1,...,p+n, j =$

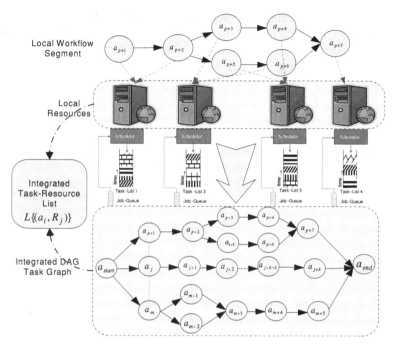

Fig. A.3 Integrated task-resource list

$1, 2, 3, 4\}$ is built and ready to be optimised.

As shown in Fig. A.2, the strategy has five major input parameters, viz. the time deficit detected at the checkpoint, the integrated Task-Resource list, the DAG task graphs which define the precedence relationships between tasks, the normal distribution models for activity durations, and resources with their execution speed and the cost per time unit. Besides, some additional information or parameters may also be required for each individual metaheuristic rescheduling algorithm. The first stage is to optimise the overall the makespan and cost for the integrated Task-Resource list through any metaheuristics based scheduling algorithm such as GA (detailed in [53]) and ACO (detailed in [51]). The first step is algorithm initialisation (Line 1) where different metaheuristic algorithms have their own initialisation process such as chromosome coding for GA and setting of initial pheromones for ACO. After initialisation, the metaheuristic algorithms are executed until the predefined stopping condition such as the maximum iteration times is met (Line 2 to Line 3). During the metaheuristic algorithms based optimisation process, a best-so-far solution can be produced in each iteration and recorded in the solution set. The second stage is to search for the best solution from the solution set (Line 5 to Line 7). During this searching stage, the occurred time deficit is first compared with the compensation time of each solution in the solution set (Line 6). Those solutions whose compensation time is smaller than the time deficit are discarded since they cannot handle the current temporal violation.

Here, the compensation time is defined as the difference between the average makespan before rescheduling and the one after rescheduling. For those remained solutions, the one with the minimum cost is returned as the best solution (Line 7 to Line 8). Finally, according to the best solution, the integrated Task-Resource list is rescheduled and deployed on related resources (Line 9).

Appendix B
Data Storage Management Strategies

Algorithm:	**Linear CTT-SP**	
Input:	Start dataset d_s; End dataset d_e;	
	A linear DDG;	//include d_s and d_e
Output:	A set of datasets in DDG	

01. For (every dataset d_i in DDG)   //Create CTT
02.   For (every dataset d_j, where $d_i \rightarrow d_j$)
03.   Create $e < d_i, d_j >$ //Create an edge
04. $weight = 0;$
05.   For (every dataset d_k, where $d_i \rightarrow d_k \rightarrow d_j$) //Calculate the weith of an edge
06. $genCost = 0;$
07.   For (every dataset d_h, where $d_i \rightarrow d_h \rightarrow d_k$)
08. $genCost = genCost + x_h ;$
09. $weight = weight + (x_k + genCost)/t_k ;$ //Accumulate generation cost rate
10. $weight = weight + y_j ;$
11.   Set $\omega < d_i, d_j >= weight;$ //Set weight to an edge
12. $P = $ Dijkstra ($d_s, d_e,$ CTT);   //Find the shortest path
13. $S = $ set of datasets that P traversed;   //Except d_s and d_e
14. Return $S;$ //The minimum cost storage stragtegy of the given linear DDG

Fig. B.1 Linear CTT-SP algorithm

X. Liu et al., *The Design of Cloud Workflow Systems*,
SpringerBriefs in Computer Science, DOI: 10.1007/978-1-4614-1933-4,
© The Author(s) 2012

Algorithm:	General_CTT-SP	
Input:	start dataset d_s; end dataset d_e;	
	a general DDG;	//Include d_s and d_e
Output:	a set of datasets in the DDG;	//The minimum cost storage strategy

01. Get a main branch MB from DDG;
02. For (every dataset d_i in MB)   //Create initial CTT
03.   For (every dataset d_j, where $d_j \in MB \wedge d_i \to d_j$)
04.   ⌐ Create $e < d_i, d_j >$;   //Create an edge
05.   │ If ($\exists d_k \in DDG \wedge d_i \nleftrightarrow d_k \wedge d_k \to d_j$)   //$e$ is an out-block edge
06.   │   Set $\omega < d_i, d_j >= \infty$;
07.   │ else   //Calculate the weight of the edge
08.   │   ⌐ weight = 0;
09.   │   │ If ($\exists d_k \notin MB \wedge d_i \to d_k \to d_j$)   //e is an over-block edge
10.   │   │   ⌐ $SB = \left\{ d_k \middle| d_k \notin MB \wedge d_i \to d_k \to d_j \right\}$;   //Get the sub-branches SB
11.   │   │   │ If (SB is linear)   //Find the minimum cost storage strategy of SB
12.   │   │   │ $S' = $ Linear_CTT-SP(d_i, d_j , SB);
13.   │   │   │ else
14.   │   │   │ $S' = $ General_CTT-SP(d_i, d_j , SB);
15.   │   │   ⌐ weight $= weight + \left(\sum_{d_i \in SB} CostR_i \right)_{S'}$;
16.   │   │   For (every dataset d_k, where $d_k \in MB \wedge d_i \to d_k \to d_j$) //Datasets in the main branch
17.   │   │   ⌐ genCost = 0;
18.   │   │   │ For (every dataset d_h, where $d_h \in MB \wedge d_i \to d_h \to d_k$)
19.   │   │   │   genCost = genCost + x_h;
20.   │   │   ⌐ weight $= weight + \left(x_k + genCost \right) / t_k$;   //Sum of generation cost rates
21.   └   └ Set $\omega < d_i, d_j >= weight + y_j$;   //Set weight to the edge
22. $CTTSet = \{ CTT_{Ini} \}$;   //Set of all the created CTTs
23. $F = \{\emptyset\}$;   //Set of datasets discovered by Dijkstra algorithm
24. While (d_e is not in F)
25.   ⌐ For (every CTT in $CTTSet$)   //Find the next edge for the shortest path
26.   │   Find the next edge by Dijkstra algorithm;
27.   │ Get the current shortest path in all the CTTs, which is with the edge $e < d_i, d_j >\in CTT'$
28.   │ Add d_j to F;
29.   │ If ($\exists d_b \in DDG \wedge d_i \to d_b \wedge d_j \nleftrightarrow d_b$)   //$e$ is an in-block edge
30.   │   ⌐ $BSet = \left\{ B_p \middle| B_p \subset DDG \wedge d_i \notin B_p \wedge d_j \in B_p \right\}$;   //The blocks that contains d_j but not d_i
31.   │   │ Create a copy of CTT' denoted as $CTT(e<d_i, d_j>)$;   //Create a new CTT for the in-block edge
32.   │   │ For (every $B_p \in BSet$)   //Update the weights of the in-block edges
33.   │   │   For (every $e < d_r, d_t >\neq e < d_i, d_j >$ where $d_r \notin B_p \wedge d_t \in B_p$)
34.   │   │   Set $\omega < d_r, d_t >= \infty$;
35.   │   │ For (every $B_p \in BSet$)   //Update the weights of the out-block edges
36.   │   │   For (every $e < d_h, d_k >$ where $d_h \in B_p \wedge d_j \to d_h \wedge d_k \notin B_p$)
37.   │   │   ⌐ weight = 0;
38.   │   │   │ $SB = \left\{ d_p \middle| d_p \in DDG \wedge d_i \to d_p \to d_k \wedge d_p \nleftrightarrow d_j \wedge d_p \nleftrightarrow d_h \right\}$;   //Get the sub-branches SB
39.   │   │   │ If (SB is linear)   //Find the minimum cost storage strategy of SB
40.   │   │   │ $S' = $ Linear_CTT-SP(d_i, d_k, SB);
41.   │   │   │ else
42.   │   │   │ $S' = $ General_CTT-SP(d_i, d_k, SB);
43.   │   │   │ weight $= \left(\sum_{d_i \in SB} CostR_i \right)_{S'}$;
44.   │   │   │ For (every dataset d_l, where $d_l \in MB \wedge d_h \to d_l \to d_k$)   //Datasets in the main branch
45.   │   │   │   ⌐ genCost = 0;
46.   │   │   │   │ For (every dataset d_o, where $d_o \in MB \wedge d_h \to d_o \to d_l$)
47.   │   │   │   │   genCost = genCost + x_o;
48.   │   │   │   ⌐ weight $= weight + \left(x_l + genCost \right) / t_l$;   //Sum of generation cost rate
49.   │   └   └ Set $\omega < d_h, d_k >= weight + y_k$;   //Set weight to the out-block edge
50.   └   Add $CTT(e<d_i, d_j>)$ to $CTTSet$;
51. Return $S = $ set of datasets that the shortest path from d_s to d_e has traversed;

Fig. B.2 General CTT-SP algorithm

Algorithm:	**Add a newly generated dataset to the DDG**
Input:	A newly generated intermediate dataset d_0 ;
	A DDG ;
Output:	Storage strategy of d_0 ;

01. **add** d_0's information to DDG ;

02. $genCost(d_0) = \left(\sum_{d_i \in d_0.pSet} d_i.t_p + d_0.t_p \right) * CostC;$ //Calculate d_0's generation cost

03. **if** ($genCost(d_0)/d_0.t > d_0.size * CostS * d_0.\lambda$)   //Compare with d_0's storage cost

04. $\{ d_0.flag = 'stored'$;   //decide to store d_0

05. $\{ d_0.CostR = d_0.size * CostS;$ //set the cost rate

06. **else**

07. $\{ d_0.flag = 'deleted'$;   //decide to delete d_0

08. $\{ d_0.CostR = genCost(d_0)/d_0.t;$ //set the cost rate

09. **update** DDG & **execute** 'store' or 'delete' on d_0 ;

Fig. B.3 Add a newly generated dataset to the DDG algorithm

Algorithm:	**Change of a stored dataset's usage frequency**
Input:	A stored intermediate dataset d_0 ;
	A DDG ;
Output:	Storage strategy of d_0 ;

01. $genCost(d_0) = \left(\sum_{d_i \in d_0.pSet} d_i.t_p + d_0.t_p \right) * CostC;$

02. **if** $\left(genCost(d_0)/d_0.t + \sum_{d_i \in d_0.fSet}(genCost(d_0)/d_i.t) > d_0.size * CostS * d_0.\lambda \right)$

03. $T' = T + d_0.t_\theta$;

04. **else**

05. $\{ d_0.flag = 'deleted'$;   //decide to delete d_0

06. $\{ d_0.CostR = genCost(d_0)/d_0.t;$ //change d_0's cost rate

07. $\{$ **for** (every d_i in $d_0.fSet$)

08. $\{$ $d_i.CostR = d_i.CostR + genCost(d_0)/d_i.t;$

09. **update** DDG & **execute** 'store' or 'delete' of d_0 ;

Fig. B.4 Change of a stored dataset's usage frequency algorithm

Algorithm: **Decide storage status of a re-generated dataset**

Input: A re-generated dataset d_0 ;

                  A DDG ;

Output: Storage strategy of d_0 and d_0's adjacent stored datasets ;

---

01. $d_0.flag = 'storted'$;   //assume d_0 is stored
02. $d_0.costR = d_0.size * costS$;   //change the cost rate of d_0
03. $\Delta = genCost(d_0)/d_0.t + \sum_{d_i \in d_0.fSet}(genCost(d_0)/d_i.t) - d_0.size * CostS * d_0.\lambda;$
04. **for** (every d_i in $d_0.fSet$)
05. $d_i.CostR = d_i.CostR - genCost(d_0)/d_i.t;$
06. **for** (every d_j directly linked by $d_0.fSet$)
07. $\ulcorner$ **if** $\left(genCost(d_j)/d_j.t + \sum_{d_m \in d_j.fSet}(genCost(d_j)/d_m.t) < d_j.size * CostS * d_j.\lambda\right)$
08. $\ulcorner$ $d_j.flag = 'deleted'$;   //decide to delete d_j
09. $\mid$ $d_j.CostR = genCost(d_j)/d_j.t;$ //change the cost rate of d_j
10. $\{$ **for** (every d_m in $d_j.fSet$)
11. $\mid$ $d_m.CostR = d_m.CostR + genCost(d_j)/d_m.t;$
12. $\llcorner$ $\llcorner$ $\Delta^+ = \Delta^+ + d_j.size * CostS - genCost(d_j)/d_j.t - \sum_{d_m \in d_j.fSet}(genCost(d_j)/d_m.t);$
13. **for** (every d_k directly linked by $d_0.pSet$)
14. $\ulcorner$ **if** $\left(genCost(d_k)/d_k.t + \sum_{d_n \in d_k.fSet}(genCost(d_k)/d_n.t) < d_k.size * CostS * d_k.\lambda\right)$
15. $\ulcorner$ $d_k.flag = 'deleted'$;   //decide to delete d_k
16. $\mid$ $d_k.CostR = genCost(d_k)/d_k.t;$
17. $\{$ **for** (every d_n in $d_k.fSet$)
18. $\mid$ $d_n.CostR = d_n.CostR + genCost(d_j)/d_n.t;$
19. $\llcorner$ $\llcorner$ $\Delta^- = \Delta^- + d_k.size * CostS - genCost(d_k)/d_k.t - \sum_{d_n \in d_k.fSet}(genCost(d_k)/d_n.t);$
20. **if** $(\Delta + \Delta^+ + \Delta^- > 0)$
21.   **update** DDG and **execute** 'store' or 'delete' on d_0 and d_0's adjacent datasets ;

Fig. B.5 Decide storage status of a re-generated dataset algorithm

Algorithm:	**Improved Linear CTT-SP**
Input:	start dataset d_s; end dataset d_e;
	a linear DDG; //Include d_s and d_e
Output:	a set of datasets in DDG

01. **for** (every dataset d_i in DDG)   //Create CTT
02.   **for** (every dataset d_j, where $d_i \rightarrow d_j$)
03. $genCost = 0$;
04.   **for** (every dataset d_u, where $d_i \rightarrow d_u \rightarrow d_j$)
05. $genCost = genCost + x_u$;
06.   **if** ($genCost/CostCPU > T_{j-1}$)
07.   **break for**;
08.   **else**
09.   Create $e < d_i, d_j >$;   //Create an edge
10. $weight = 0$;
11.   **for** (every dataset d_k, where $d_i \rightarrow d_k \rightarrow d_j$)
12. $genCost = 0$;
13.   **for** (every dataset d_h, where $d_i \rightarrow d_h \rightarrow d_k$)
14. $genCost = genCost + x_h$;
15. $weight = weight + (x_k + genCost) * v_k$;
16. $weight = weight + y_j * \lambda_j$;
17.   Set $\omega < d_i, d_j >= weight$;   //Set weight to an edge
18. $P_{\min} < d_s, d_e > =$ Dijkstra_Algorithm (d_s, d_e, CTT);
19. $S =$ set of datasets that $P_{\min} < d_s, d_e >$ traversed;
20. Return S;   //Storing S is the minimum cost storage strategy

Fig. B.6 Improved CTT-SP algorithm

Appendix C
Replication Management Strategies

Cost-effective Incremental Replication

Input: *DS*: the set of data; *X*: reliability requirement
FRS: failure rate set

```
1.     Initialisation {
2.        T<-new Array[1,3];              // initialise the output set to an empty 1*3 array.
3.        time<-0;                        // initialise the time counter
4.        NRCTP<-0;                       // initialise the record of next replica creation time point
5.        U<-DS.storageUnit();            // get the first storage unit in which the original data is stored
6.        FR<-find the failure rate of U in FRS;
7.        add FR to SFRS;                 // SFRS: sub failure rate set recording storage unit for each replica
8.        k<-1; }                         // initialise the replica number counter

9.     Start {                           // main body of CIR
10.       time.startToCount();            // start to count the storage duration
11.       while (!DS.isStorageFinished() & k<=3) {   // CIR will not stop until the data has been changed or the maximum
                                                     // number of replicas has been reached
12.         if (k=1) {
13.           <-get the element from SFRS;            // there is only one element in SFRS now
14.           solve function;             // Function (2)
15.           <- find the positive real root of // obtain the duration
16.           NRCTP<-NRCTP-;              // update the next replica creation time point
17.           T[1,1]<- ; }               //end if.
18.         if (k=2) {
19.           <-all two elements from SFRS;
20.           solve function ; //Function (3)
21.           a<- find the positive real root of ;
22.           <-;                        //solve the function in two steps and obtain
23.           NRCTP<-NRCTP-;
24.           T[1,2]<-; }                // end if.
25.         if (k=3) {
26.           <-all three elements from SFRS;
27.           solve function;
28.           b<- find the positive real root of ;  // Function (4)
29.           <-;
30.           NRCTP<-NRCTP-1;
31.           T[1,3]<-; }   // end if.
32.         k<-k+1;                       // update the replica counter
33.         wait until time=NRCTP; //this process will re-activate until next replica creation time point
34.         if (k!=3) {
35.           U <-DS.getNewStorageUnit();
36.           create a new replica for DS in U;
37.           FR<-find the failure rate of U in FRS;
38.           SFRS<-SFRS+FR; } } } //create one more replica for the data if current replica number is lower than 3.
                                   //End if. End while. End Start.
```

Fig. C.1 Pseudo-code of CIR strategy

X. Liu et al., *The Design of Cloud Workflow Systems,*
SpringerBriefs in Computer Science, DOI: 10.1007/978-1-4614-1933-4,
© The Author(s) 2012

We take an example to illustrate how CIR works. Consider the most common case that a set of data is newly received at time point 0 and stored using the default mode. In the initialisation stage of the storage process (Lines 1–8), the reliability requirement is initialised to a certain value, e.g. 99.99%, and the replica number starts from 1. After the initialisation is finished, the process for calculating the replica creation time points is activated (Lines 9–38) and starts to calculate the first replica creation time point: the first replica creation time point is the positive real root of Function (2) in Sect. 4.6.2 (Lines 12–17). Assume the storage unit u_1 has a failure rate of λ_1, by solving Function (2), the first replica creation time point T_1 can be obtained. When the first replica creation time point is reached, the process for calculating the second time point will start. Similarly, by solving Function (3) in Sect. 4.6.2 (Lines 18–24), T_2 can be obtained and the second round of the algorithm should start at T_1+T_2. This process continues until the data has been changed or the maximum number of replicas reached or data loss happens (Line 11). At this stage of the process, there are three replicas stored in the system. Then, at the end, by solving Function (4) in Sect. 4.6.2 (Lines 25–31), the storage duration of the three replica stage can be derived. In the case of data loss which is another important part in data management area, the corresponding research is beyond the scope of this chapter.

Appendix D
Trust-Based Noise Injection Strategy

Title: Trusted-based noise injection strategy	
Input: Service-request query Q_U	
Output: Generated noise for service-request query Q_N and noise injected intensity ε	
Step 1: Evaluating the trust relation	Input: p and q denote two roles: service-request initiator and service-request respondent in the trust relation
	Output: v denotes the trust value between p and q, in the range of [0,1]
	We have trust relations: $TR = \{tr_1, tr_2, ..., tr_i, ..., tr_m\}$ and $tr_i = (P_i, Q_i, C_i, T_i, D_i, t_i, v_i, p_i, n_i)$. Check all t_i in tr_i, remove all tr_i with unavailable t_i. Check all i which can satisfy $P_i == p$ and $Q_i == q$. If i not existed, Dijkstra Algorithm is used to find out an array of trusts, and a new derived tr will be inserted in to TR. Then this step will re-run. If i existed, if i is unique, so $v = v_i$. if i is not unique, $v = v_j$ (which $j \in$ the dataset of i and $T_j == direct$)
Step 2: Evaluating privacy in the service-request query	Input: tr_i denotes the trust relation in the service-request query, $d \in \{$serious, moderate, slight$\}$ which denotes the privacy risk from the customer's judgement.
	Output: $d' \in \{$serious, moderate, slight$\}$ which denotes the privacy risk in this architecture.
	Check D_i from tr_i. If (D_i==customer-control), $d' = d$. If (D_i==control–control), $d' = d$. If (D_i== control-public), if ($d ==$ slight), $d' =$ moderate. if ($.d! = .$slight), $d' = d$. From original data query to privacy, we set three levels to classify privacy. $pl = \{$directly privacy, distributed features, interaction features$\}$. To get $d \in \{$serious, moderate, slight$\}$, the user's judgement bases on the protection requirements for different levels of privacy. They correspond one by one

(continued)

X. Liu et al., *The Design of Cloud Workflow Systems*,
SpringerBriefs in Computer Science, DOI: 10.1007/978-1-4614-1933-4,
© The Author(s) 2012

(continued)

Step 3: Settling down noise injected intensity, and generating the noise to inject into service-request query	Input: Q_U, d', v
	
	Output: Q_N denoted by $P(Q_N = q_i)$, $\forall i$, ε denotes noise injected intensity
	
	3.1 Settle down the noise generated strategy
	If ($d' ==$ slight), jumping to step 3.2, and slight noise generated strategy will be applied.
	If ($d' ==$ moderate), jumping to step 3.3, the moderate noise generated strategy will be applied.
	If ($d' ==$ serious), jumping to step 3.4, the serious noise generated strategy will be applied.
	These three strategies will be discussed in next
	
	3.2 Slight noise generated strategy (the goal of this strategy is to confuse directly privacy)
	This strategy is random noise with $P(Q_N = q_i) = \frac{1}{n}$, $\forall i$, and n is the size of range of Q_N and Q_U.
	The key of this strategy is the noise injected intensity, we set $\varepsilon = 1 - v$. Jump to Step 4
	
	3.3 Moderate noise generated strategy (the goal of this strategy is to confuse distributed features privacy)
	To match the goal of this strategy, we generate noise to make the injected result with confused distributed features by
	$$P(Q_N = q_i) = \frac{Max\{P(Q_U=q_i)\}-P(Q_U=q_i)}{n*Max\{P(Q_U=q_i)\}-\sum_i P(Q_U=q_i)}, \forall i.$$
	We set
	$$\varepsilon' = 2(1 - v)\frac{n*Max\{P(Q_U=q_i)\}-\sum_i P(Q_U=q_i)}{n*Max\{P(Q_U=q_i)\}}$$ to match the noise can fulfil its function
	And the final $\varepsilon = Max\{\varepsilon', 1 - v\}$. Jump to Step 4
	
	3.4 Serious noise generated strategy (the goal of this strategy is to confuse interaction features privacy)
	To match the goal of this strategy, we generate noise to make the injected result with confused interaction features by
	$$P(Q_N = q_i) = \frac{Max\{P(Q_S=q_i)\}-P(Q_S=q_i)}{n*Max\{P(Q_S=q_i)\}-\sum_i P(Q_S=q_i)}, \forall i.$$
	We set
	$$\varepsilon(t) = 2(1 - v)\frac{n*Max\{P[Q_S(t)=q_i]\}-\sum_i P[Q_S(t)=q_i]}{n*Max\{P[Q_S(t)=q_i]\}}.$$
	The final $\varepsilon = Max\{\varepsilon(t), 1 - v\}$ and it changes with time t passing. Jump to Step 4.

Step 4: Evaluating the quality of this service process, and updating trust relation in trust model about this service process	Input: e denotes the quality evaluation of this service process from service-request initiator which is the one generating the noise.
	
	Output: updated tr_i
	4.1 Get the feedback e from the service-request initiator.
	4.2 Update the p_i or n_i in tr_i
	If (($e > v_i$), $p_i = p_i + 1$
	If ($e < v_i$), $n_i = n_i + 1$
	4.3 Update v_i in tr_i
	$v_i = v_i + e \times (p_i - n_i)$

In this strategy, there are three noise generated strategies which achieve noise generation process.

It is necessary to discuss the difference between serious noise generated strategy and moderate noise generated strategy. In step 3.3 and 3.4 of this strategy, their noise generated formulas are $P(Q_N = q_i) = \frac{Max\{P(Q_U=q_i)\}-P(Q_U=q_i)}{n*Max\{P(Q_U=q_i)\}-\sum_i P(Q_U=q_i)}, \forall i$ and $P(Q_N = q_i) = \frac{Max\{P(Q_S=q_i)\}-P(Q_S=q_i)}{n*Max\{P(Q_S=q_i)\}-\sum_i P(Q_S=q_i)}, \forall i$. The $P(Q_U = q_i)$ changes to $P(Q_S = q_i)$. It means that serious noise generated strategy is more sensitive to the time element, and it is the found of the goal of serious noise generated strategy to keep interaction's frequency.

Another issue should be clarified is $\varepsilon(t)$ and $Q_S(t)$ in the noise injected intensity formula $\varepsilon(t) = (1 - v)\frac{n*Max\{P[Q_S(t)=q_i]\}-\sum_i P[Q_S(t)=q_i]}{n*Max\{P[Q_S(t)=q_i]\}}$. It is the development of the former issue to fulfil the goal of serious noise generated strategy by involve time *t*element.

The last issue is that εgeneration in these three strategies. With the risk level rises, one noise generated strategy covers the former one. It comes from $\varepsilon = v$, $\varepsilon = Max\{\varepsilon', 1 - v\}$, to $\varepsilon = Max\{\varepsilon(t), 1 - v\}$.

In summary, this strategy for privacy protection in cloud establishes on the background of trust model and noise injection model in cloud, operates in the noise injection architecture, and protects privacy during whole privacy transaction process in cloud environments, especially in cloud workflow instances.

Appendix E
Literature Review

Since the research on cloud workflow management systems is at its early stage, it is difficult to conduct direct comparison between SwinDeW-C with others at present. Most of the current projects are either on the general implementation of cloud computing or focus on some specific aspects such as data management in the cloud. There exists some research into data-intensive applications on the cloud [60], such as early experiences like Nimbus [42] and Cumulus [78] projects. Comparing to the distributed computing systems like cluster and grid, a cloud computing system has a cost benefit [8]. Assunção et al. [9] demonstrate that cloud computing can extend the capacity of clusters with a cost benefit. Using Amazon clouds' cost model and BOINC volunteer computing middleware, the work in [44] analyses the cost benefit of cloud computing versus grid computing. In terms of the cost benefit, the work by Deelman et al. [27] shows that cloud computing offers a cost-effective solution for data-intensive applications, such as scientific workflows [38]. The work in [38] explores the use of cloud computing for scientific workflows, focusing on a widely used astronomy application-Montage. The Cloudbus project (http://www.gridbus.org/cloudbus/) is working on a new generalised and extensible cloud simulation framework named CloudSim [19] which can enable seamless modelling, simulation, and experimentation of cloud computing infrastructures and management services.

With the existing projects for many grid workflow systems developed in recent years, it is agreed by many researchers and practitioners that cloud workflow systems might be built on grid computing environments rather than from scratch. For example, the CloudSim toolkit used in the Cloudbus project is implemented by programmatically extending the core functionalities exposed by the GridSim used in the Gridbus project (http://www.gridbus.org). Therefore, we review some representative grid workflow system and focus on the related features discussed in this paper such as workflow scheduling architecture, QoS, data and security management. Specifically, we investigate Gridbus, Pegasus (http://pegasus.isi.edu/), Taverna (http://www.taverna.org.uk/), GrADS (http://www.iges.org/grads/), ASKALON

X. Liu et al., *The Design of Cloud Workflow Systems*,
SpringerBriefs in Computer Science, DOI: 10.1007/978-1-4614-1933-4,
© The Author(s) 2012

(http://www.askalon.org/), GridAnt (http://www.globus.org/cog/projects/gridant/), Triana (http://www.trianacode.org/), GridFlow (http://gridflow.ca/) and Kepler (https://kepler-project.org/). For the architecture of the workflow scheduling, Pegasus, Taverna, GrADS, and Kepler use a centralised architecture; Gridbus and GridFlow use a hierarchical architecture; ASKALON and Triana use a decentralised architecture. It is believed that centralised schemes produce more efficient schedules and decentralised schemes have better scalabilities, while hierarchical schemes are their compromises. Similar to SwinDeW-G, SwinDeW-C uses a structured decentralised scheme for workflow scheduling. SwinDeW-G aims at using a performance-driven strategy to achieve an overall load balance of the whole system via distributing tasks to least loaded neighbours.

As far as QoS (quality of service) constraints are concerned, most grid workflow systems mentioned above do not support this feature. Gridbus supports QoS constraints including task deadline and cost minimisation, GrADS and GridFlow mainly use estimated application execution time, and ASKALON supports constrains and properties specified by users or predefined. Right now, SwinDeW-C supports QoS constraints based on task deadlines. When it comes to fault tolerance, at the task level, Gridbus, Taverna, ASKALON, Karajan, GridFlow and Kepler use alternate resource; Taverna, ASKALON and Karajan use retry; GrADS uses rescheduling. At the workflow level, rescue workflow is used by ASKALON and Kepler; user-defined exception handling is used by Karajan and Kepler. Pegasus, GridAnt and Triana use their particular strategies respectively. As a comparison, SwinDeW-C uses effective temporal constraint verification for detecting and handling temporal violations.

As for data management, Kepler has its own actor-oriented data modelling method that for large data in the grid environment. It has two Grid actors, called FileFetcher and FileStager, respectively. These actors make use of GridFTP to retrieve files from, or move files to, remote locations on the Grid. Pegasus has developed some data placement algorithms in the grid environment and uses the RLS (Replica Location Service) system as data management at runtime. In Pegasus, data are asynchronously moved to the tasks on demand to reduce the waiting time of the execution and dynamically delete the data that the task no longer needs to reduce the use of storage. In Gridbus, the workflow system has several scheduling algorithms for the data-intensive applications in the grid environment based on a Grid Resource Broker. The algorithms are designed based on different theories (GA, MDP, SCP, Heuristic), to adapt to different use cases. Taverna proposed a new process definition language, Sculf, which could model application data in a dataflow. It considers workflow as a graph of processors, each of which transfers a set of data inputs into a set of data outputs. ASKALON is a workflow system designed for scheduling. It puts the computing overhead and data transfer overhead together to get a value "weight". It dose not discriminate the computing resource and data host. ASKALON also has its own process definition language called AGWL. Triana is a workflow system which is based on a problem-solving environment that enables the data-intensive scientific application to execute. For the grid, it has an independent abstraction middleware layer, called the Grid Application Prototype (GAP), enables users to advertise, discover and communicate with Web and peer-to-peer (p2p) services. Triana also uses the RLS to manage data at runtime. GridFlow is a workflow system which uses an agent-based system for grid resource management. It considers data transfer to computing resources and archive to storage resources as kinds of workflow tasks.

As for security management, Globus uses public key cryptography (also known as asymmetric cryptography) as the basis for its security management, which represents the main stream in the grid security area. Globus uses the certificates encoded in the X.509 certificate format, an established standard data format. These certificates can be shared among public key based software, including commercial Web browsers from Microsoft and Netscape. The International Grid Trust Federation (IGTF) (http://www.igtf.net/) is a third-party grid trust service provider which aims to establish common policies and guidelines between its Policy Management Authorities (PMAs) members. The IGTF does not provide identity assertions but ensures that within the scope of the IGTF charter, the assertions issued by accredited authorities of any of its PMAs member can meet or exceed an authentication profile relevant to the accredited authority. The European GridTrust project (http://www.gridtrust.eu/gridtrust/) is a novel and ambitious project, which provides new security services at the GRID middleware layer. GridTrust is developing a Usage Control Service to monitor resource usage in dynamic Virtual Organisations (VO), enforce usage policies at run-time, and report usage control policy violations. This service brings dynamic usage control to Grid security in traditional, rigid authorisation models. Other services of the security framework include a Grid Security Requirements editor to allow VO owners and users to define security policies; a Secure-Aware Resource Broker Service to help create VOs based on services with compatible security policies; and a sophisticated Reputation Manager Service, to record past behaviour of VO owners and users as reputation credentials.

Bibliography

1. Australian Academy of Technology Science and Engineering, Cloud Computing: Opportunities and Challenges for Australia. http://www.atse.org.au/component/remository/ATSE-Reports/Information-Technology/CLOUD-COMPUTING-Opportunities-and-Challenges-for-Australia-2010/. Accessed 1 Aug 2011
2. Aalst, W.M.P., van der Hee, K.M.V.: Workflow Management: Models, Methods and Systems. The MIT Press, Cambridge (2002)
3. Alexandru, I.: Performance analysis of cloud computing services for many-tasks scientific computing. IEEE Trans. Parallel Distributed Syst. **22**(6), 931–945 (2011)
4. Deutsch A, Papakonstantinou Y, Privacy in database publishing. In: 10th International Conference on Database Theory, pp. 230–245 (2005)
5. Alonso, G., Günthör, R., Kamath, M., Agrawal, D., El Abbadi, A., Mohan, C.: Exotica/FMDC: a workflow management system for mobile and disconnected clients. Distributed Parallel Databases **4**, 229–247 (1996)
6. Pereira, A.L., Muppavarapu, V., Chung S.M.,: Role-based access control for grid database services using the community authorization service. IEEE Trans. Dependable Secure Comput. **3**, 156–166 (2006)
7. Ardagna, D., Pernici, B.: Adaptive service composition in flexible processes. IEEE Trans. Softw. Eng. **33**, 369–384 (2007)
8. Armbrust, M., Fox, A., Griffith, R., Joseph, A.D., Katz, R.H., Konwinski, A., Lee, G., Patterson, D.A., Rabkin, A., Stoica, I., Zaharia, M.: Above the clouds: a Berkeley view of cloud computing. Technical report, UCB/EECS-2009-28, University of California, Berkeley (2009)
9. Assuncao, M.D.d., Costanzo, A.d., Buyya, R.: Evaluating the cost-benefit of using cloud computing to extend the capacity of clusters. In: 18th ACM International Symposium on High Performance Distributed Computing, pp. 1–10 (2009)
10. Australian Government Department of Finance and Deregulation: Cloud Computing Strategic Direction Paper. http://www.finance.gov.au/e-government/strategy-and-governance/cloud-computing.html. Accessed 1 Aug 2011
11. Australian Government, Department of the Environment, Water, Heritage and the Arts: Australian Government ICT Sustainability Plan. http://www.environment.gov.au/sustainability/government/ictplan/publications/plan/index.html. Accessed 1 Aug 2011
12. Barr J., Varia J., Wood M.: Animoto - Scaling Through Viral Growth. http://aws.typepad.com/aws/2008/04/animoto—scali.html. Accessed 1 Aug 2011
13. Bhargav-spantzel, A., Squicciarini, A.C., Bertino, E.: Trust negotiation in identity management. IEEE Security Privacy **5**, 55–63 (2007)

X. Liu et al., *The Design of Cloud Workflow Systems*,
SpringerBriefs in Computer Science, DOI: 10.1007/978-1-4614-1933-4,
© The Author(s) 2012

14. Borthakur, D.: The hadoop distributed file system: architecture and design. http://hadoop.
    apache.org/common/docs/r0.18.3/hdfs_design.html. Accessed 1 Aug 2011
15. Bose, R., Frew, J.: Lineage retrieval for scientific data processing: a survey. ACM Comput.
    Surv. **37**, 1–28 (2005)
16. Boss, G., Malladi, P., Quan, D., Legregni, L., Hall, H.: IBM cloud computing (White Paper)
    (2007)
17. Buyya, R., Yeo, C.S., Venugopal, S., Broberg, J., Brandic, I.: Cloud computing and emerging
    IT platforms: vision, hype, and reality for delivering computing as the 5th utility. Future
    Gener. Comput. Syst. **25**, 599–616 (2009)
18. Cai, T., Gloor, P.A., Nog, S.: DartFlow: A Workflow Management System on the Web Using
    Transportable Agents. Dartmouth College, Hanover (1996)
19. Calheiros, R.N., Ranjan, R., Rose, C.A.F.D., Buyya, R.: CloudSim: A Novel Framework for
    Modeling and Simulation of Cloud Computing Infrastructures and Services. Grid Computing
    and Distributed Systems (GRIDS) Laboratory, Technical report. Department of Computer
    Science and Software Engineering, The University of Melbourne (2009)
20. Cardoso, J.: Stochastic workflow reduction algorithm. Technical report, LSDIS Lab,
    Department of Computer Science, University of Georgia (2002)
21. Chen, J., Yang, Y.: Multiple states based temporal consistency for dynamic verification of
    fixed-time constraints in grid workflow systems. Concurr. Comput.: Pract. Experience **19**,
    965–982 (2007)
22. Chen, J., Yang, Y.: Temporal dependency based checkpoint selection for dynamic
    verification of temporal constraints in scientific workflow systems. ACM Trans. Softw.
    Eng. Methodol. **20**(3), article 9 (2011)
23. Chen, J., Yang, Y.: Adaptive selection of necessary and sufficient checkpoints for dynamic
    verification of temporal constraints in grid workflow systems. ACM Trans. Auton. Adapt.
    Syst. **2**, article 6 (2007)
24. Chen, J., Yang, Y.: Temporal dependency based checkpoint selection for dynamic
    verification of fixed-time constraints in grid workflow systems. In: 30th International
    Conference on Software Engineering, pp. 141–150 (2008)
25. Lin, C., Varadharajan, V., Wang, Y., Pruthi, V.: Enhancing grid security with trust
    management. In: 2004 IEEE International Conference on Services Computing, pp. 303–310
    (2004)
26. Coulouris, G., Dollimore, J., Kindberg, T.: Distributed Systems: Concepts and Design, 4th
    edn. Pearson Education Limited, Harlow (2005)
27. Deelman, E., Gannon, D., Shields, M., Taylor, I.: Workflows and e-science: an overview of
    workflow system features and capabilities. Future Gener. Comput. Syst. **25**, 528–540 (2008)
28. Dogac, A., Gokkoca, E., Arpinar, S., Koksal, P., Cingil, I., Arpinar, B., Tatbul, N., Karagoz,
    P., Halici, U., Altinel, M.: Design and implementation of a distributed workflow management
    system: METUFlow. In: Doğaç, A., Kalinichenko, L., Özsu, M.T., Sheth, A. (eds.) Workflow
    Management Systems and Interoperability, pp. 61–91 (1998)
29. Erl, T.: SOA: Principles of Service Design. Prentice Hall, London (2008)
30. European Commission, The Future of Cloud Computing, Opportunities for European Cloud
    Computing Beyond 2010. http://cordis.europa.eu/fp7/ict/ssai/docs/cloud-report-final.pdf.
    Accessed 1 Aug 2011
31. Ferretti, S., Ghini, V., Panzieri, F., Pellegrini, M., Turrini, E.: QoS-Aware clouds. In: 3rd
    IEEE International Conference on Cloud Computing, pp. 321–328 (2010)
32. Foster, I., Yong, Z., Raicu, I., Lu, S.: Cloud computing and grid computing 360-degree
    compared. In: Grid Computing Environments Workshop, pp. 1–10 (2008)
33. Zhang G., Yang Y., Yuan D., Chen J.: A trust-based noise injection strategy for privacy
    protection in cloud computing. Software: practice and experience, Wiley, to appear.
    www.ict.swin.edu.au/personal/yyang/papers/SPE-privacy-2010.pdf. Accessed 1 Aug 2011
34. Gartner: Gartner says worldwide cloud services revenue will grow 21.3 percent in 2009.
    http://www.gartner.com/it/page.jsp?id=920712. Accessed 1 Aug 2011

35. Ghemawat, S., Gobioff, H., Leung, S.-T.: The Google file system. SIGOPS Oper. Syst. Rev. **37**, 29–43 (2003)
36. Gottfrid D.: Self-service, prorated supercomputing fun. http://open.blogs.nytimes. com/2007/11/01/self-service-prorated-super-computing-fun/. Accessed 1 Aug 2011
37. Grundy, J.C., Apperley, M.D., Hosking, J.G., Mugridge, W.B.: A decentralized architecture for software process modeling and enactment. IEEE Internet Comput. **2**, 53–62 (1998)
38. Hoffa, C., Mehta, G., Freeman, T., Deelman, E., Keahey, K., Berriman, B., Good, J.: On the use of cloud computing for scientific workflows. In: 4th IEEE International Conference on e-Science, pp. 640–645 (2008)
39. IBM, Understanding quality of service for web services. http://www.ibm.com/ developerworks/library/ws-quality.html. Accessed 1 Aug 2011
40. Juve, G., Deelman, E., Vahi, K., Mehta, G., Berriman, B., Berman, P.B., Maechling, P.: Scientific workflow applications on amazon EC2. In: Workshop on Cloud-based Services and Applications in conjunction with 5th IEEE International Conference on e-Science, pp. 59–66 (2009)
41. Kao, B., Garcia-Molina, H.: Deadline assignment in a distributed soft real-time system. IEEE Trans. Parallel Distributed Syst. **8**, 1268–1274 (1997)
42. Keahey, K., Figueiredo, R., Fortes, J., Freeman, T., Tsugawa, M.: Science clouds: early experiences in cloud computing for scientific applications. In: First Workshop on Cloud Computing and its Applications, pp. 1–6 (2008)
43. Khodakaram-Salimifard, M.W.: Petri-net based modelling of workflow systems: an overview. Eur. J. Oper. Res. **134**, 664–676 (2001)
44. Kondo, D., Javadi, B., Malecot, P., Cappello, F., Anderson, D.P.: Cost-benefit analysis of cloud computing versus desktop grids. In: IEEE International Symposium on Parallel and Distributed Processing, pp. 1-12 (2009)
45. Krutz, R.L., Vines, R.D.: Cloud Security: A Comprehensive Guide to Secure Cloud Computing. Wiley, New York (2010)
46. Liangzhao, Z., Benatallah, B., Ngu, A.H.H., Dumas, M., Kalagnanam, J., Chang, H.: QoS-aware middleware for web services composition. IEEE Trans. Softw. Eng. **30**, 311–327 (2004)
47. Liu, K., Jin, H., Chen, J., Liu, X., Yuan, D., Yang, Y.: A compromised-time-cost scheduling algorithm in SwinDeW-C for instance-intensive cost-constrained workflows on cloud computing platform. Int. J. High Perform. Comput. Appl. **24**(4), 445–456 (2010)
48. Liu, X., Chen, J., Wu, Z., Ni, Z., Yuan, D., Yang, Y.: Handling recoverable temporal violations in scientific workflow systems: a workflow rescheduling based strategy. In: 10th IEEE/ACM International Symposium on Cluster, Cloud and Grid Computing, pp. 534–537 (2010)
49. Liu, X., Chen, J., Yang, Y.: A probabilistic strategy for setting temporal constraints in scientific workflows. In: 6th International Conference on Business Process Management, pp. 180–195 (2008)
50. Liu, X., Ni, Z., Chen, J., Yang, Y.: A probabilistic strategy for temporal constraint management in scientific workflow systems. Concurr. Comput: Pract. Experience **23**(16), 1893–1919 (2011)
51. Liu, X., Ni, Z., Wu, Z., Yuan, D., Chen, J., Yang, Y.: A novel general framework for automatic and cost-effective handling of recoverable temporal violations in scientific workflow systems. J. Syst. Softw. **84**(3), 492–509 (2011a)
52. Liu, X., Ni, Z., Yuan, D., Jiang, y., Wu, Z., Chen, J., Yang, Y.: A novel statistical time-series pattern based interval forecasting strategy for activity durations in workflow systems. J. Syst. Softw. **84**(3), 354–376 (2011b)
53. Liu, X., Yang, Y., Jiang, Y., Chen, J.: Preventing temporal violations in scientific workflows: where and how. IEEE Trans. Softw. Eng. doi:ieeecomputersociety.org/10.1109/TSE.2010.99. Accessed 1 Aug 2011

54. Liu, X., Yuan, D., Zhang, G., Chen, J., Yang, Y.: SwinDeW-C: a peer-to-peer based cloud workflow system. In: Furht, B., Escalante, A. (eds.) Handbook of Cloud Computing. Springer, Heidelberg (2010b)
55. Ludascher, B., Altintas, I., Berkley, C., Higgins, D., Jaeger, E., Jones, M., Lee, E.A.: Scientific workflow management and the Kepler system. Concurr. Comput: Pract. Experience **18**, 1039–1065 (2005)
56. Mark, D.: Ryan: cloud computing privacy concerns on our doorstep. Commun. ACM **54**, 36–38 (2011)
57. McCormick, W.T., Sehweitzer, P.J., White, T.W.: Problem decomposition and data reorganization by a clustering technique. Oper. Res. **20**, 993–1009 (1972)
58. Greer, M.B. Jr.: Software as a Service Inflection Point. iUniverse (2009)
59. Moore, M.: An accurate parallel genetic algorithm to schedule tasks on a cluster. Parallel Comput. **30**, 567–583 (2004)
60. Moretti, C., Bulosan, J., Thain, D., Flynn, P.J.: All-Pairs: an abstraction for data-intensive cloud computing. In: IEEE International Parallel and Distributed Processing Symposium, pp. 1–11 (2008)
61. Nurmi, D., Wolski, R., Grzegorczyk, C.: Eucalyptus : A technical report on an elastic utility computing archietcture linking your programs to useful systems. UCSB Computer Science Technical Report (2008)
62. Pandey, S., Karunamoorthy, D., Buyya, R.: Workflow engine for clouds. In: Buyya, R., Broberg, J., Goscinski, A.M. (eds.) Cloud Computing: Principles and Paradigms. Wiley, New York (2011)
63. Paul, S., Park, E., Chaar, J.: RainMan: a workflow system for the internet. In: USENIX Symposium on Internet Technologies and System, pp. 15–15 (1997)
64. Poniatowski, M.: Foundations of Green IT. Prentice Hall, London (2010)
65. Raghavan, B., Vishwanath, K.V., Ramabhadran, S., Yocum, K., Snoeren. A.C.: Cloud control with distributed rate limiting. In: Proceedings of 2007 ACM SIGCOMM, pp. 337–348 (2007)
66. Richard, E.B.: A Bayes explanation of an apparent failure rate paradox. IEEE Trans. Reliab. **34**, 107–108 (1985)
67. Rosenberg, F., Curbera, F., Duftler, M.J., Khalaf, R.: Composing RESTful services and collaborative workflows—a lightweight approach. IEEE Internet Comput. **12**, 24–31 (2008)
68. Russell, N., van der Aalst, W.M.P., Hofstede, A.H.M.t.: Exception handling patterns in process-aware information systems. Technical Report, BPMcenter.org (2006)
69. Russell, N., van der Aalst, W.M.P., Hofstede, A.H.M.t.: Workflow exception patterns. In: 18th International Conference on Advanced Information Systems Engineering, pp. 288–302 (2006)
70. SECES: In: First International Workshop on Software Engineering for Computational Science and Engineering, in conjuction with the 30th International Conference on Software Engineering (2008)
71. Serhani, M.A., Dssouli, R., Hafid, A., Sahraoui, H.: A QoS broker based architecture for efficient Web services selection. In: 2005 IEEE International Conference on Web Services, pp. 113–120 (2005)
72. Simmhan, Y.L., Plale, B., Gannon, D.: A survey of data provenance in e-science. SIGMOD Record 34, pp. 31–36 (2005)
73. Sosinsky, B.: Cloud Computing Bible. Wiley, New York (2010)
74. Taylor, I.J., Deelman, E., Gannon, D.B., Shields, M.: Workflows for e-Science: Scientific Workflows for Grids. Springer, Heidelberg (2007)
75. Vecchiola, C., Chu, X., Buyya, R.: Aneka: A software platform for.NET-based cloud computing. In: 2008 High Performance Computing Workshop, pp. 267–295 (2008)
76. Wang C., Wang Q., Ren K., Lou W.: Ensuring data storage security in cloud computing. In: 17th IEEE International Workshop on Quality of Service, pp. 1–9 (2009)
77. Wang, L., Jie, W., Chen, J. (eds.): Grid Computing: Infrastructure, Service, and Applications. CRC Press, Talyor & Francis Group, Boca Raton (2009)

78. Wang, L.H., Kunze, M., Tao, J.: Performance evaluation of virtual machine-based grid workflow system. Concurr. Comput.: Pract. Experience **20**(15), 1759–1771 (2008)
79. Weiss, A.: Computing in the cloud. ACM Networker **11**, 18–25 (2007)
80. White, T.: Haddop the Definite Guide. O'Reilly Media, Sebastopol (2009)
81. Winsborough, W.H., Li, N.: Safety in automated trust negotiation. ACM Trans. Inf. Syst. Secur. **9**, 352–390 (2006)
82. Workflow Management Coalition: The Workflow Reference Model, WFMC-TC-1003 (1995)
83. Wu, Z., Liu, X., Ni, Z., Yuan, D., Yang, Y.: A market-oriented hierarchical scheduling strategy in cloud workflow systems. J Supercomput. http://dx.doi.org/10.1007/s11227-011-0578-4. Accessed 1 Aug 2011
84. Yan, J., Yang, Y., Raikundalia, G.K.: SwinDeW—a peer-to-peer based decentralized workflow management system. IEEE Trans. Systems, Man and Cybernetics, Part A **36**, 922–935 (2006)
85. Yang, Y., Liu, K., Chen, J., Lignier, J., Jin, H.: Peer-to-peer based grid workflow runtime environment of SwinDeW-G. In: 3rd International Conference on e-Science and Grid Computing, pp. 51–58 (2007)
86. Young, J.W.: A first order approximation to the optimal checkpoint interval. Commun. ACM **17**, 530–531 (1974)
87. Yu, J., Buyya, R.: A taxonomy of Workflow Management Systems for Grid Computing. J. Grid Comput. **3**(3–4), 171–200 (2005)
88. Yuan, D., Yang, Y., Liu, X., Chen, J.: A cost-effective strategy for intermediate data storage in scientific cloud workflow systems. In: 24th IEEE International Parallel and Distributed Processing Symposium, pp. 1–12 (2010)
89. Yuan, D., Yang, Y., Liu, X., Chen, J.: A local-optimisation based strategy for cost-effective datasets storage of scientific applications in the cloud. In: IEEE International Conference on Cloud Computing, pp. 179–186 (2011)
90. Yuan, D., Yang, Y., Liu, X., Chen, J.:On-demand minimum cost benchmarking for intermediate datasets storage in scientific cloud workflow systems. J. Parallel Distrib. Comput. **72**, 316–332 (2011)
91. Yuan, D., Yang, Y., Liu, X., Zhang, G., Chen, J.: A data dependency based strategy for intermediate data storage in scientific cloud workflow systems. Concurr. Comput.: Pract. Experience. http://onlinelibrary.wiley.com/doi/10.1002/cpe.1636/pdf. Accessed 1 Aug 2011
92. Zaharia, M., Konwinski, A., Joseph, A.D., Katz, R., Stoica, I.: Improving MapReduce performance in heterogeneous environments. In: 8th USENIX Symposium on Operating Systems Design and Implementation, pp. 29–42 (2008)